781   Evans, Roger
EVA
        How to read music

              1903

DATE		
OCT. 28 1983		
MY 23 '86		
MR 27 '87		
AP 02 '90		
MR 05 '96		
FE 29 00		
APR 25 '05		
FEB 05 '07		
FEB 22 '07		

© THE BAKER & TAYLOR CO.

HOW TO
READ MUSIC

HOW TO
READ MUSIC

for Singing, Guitar, Piano, Organ and Most Instruments

Roger Evans

CROWN PUBLISHERS, INC.
NEW YORK

First published in Great Britain 1978
by Elm Tree Books Ltd
90 Great Russell Street, London WC1B 3PT

in association with

EMI Music Publishing Ltd
138-140 Charing Cross Road, London WC2H 0LD

First published in the U.S.A. 1979
by Crown Publishers, Inc., New York

Library of Congress Cataloging in Publication Data

Evans, Roger.
   How to read music.

   1. Music—Instruction and study. 2. Sight-reading
(Music) I. Title.
MT35.E88   1979   781'.24   79-20844
ISBN: 0-517-538970
10 9 8 7 6 5 4 3 2

Design and production in association with Book Production Consultants
Printed in U.S.A.

Contents

Introduction

It's the same in Australia, Britain, France, Germany, Italy, Russia, Scandinavia, South America, Spain, U.S.A. and most countries in the world.

. . . and the same for Classical, Popular, Folk, Jazz and most types of music.

It's the same for singing, the guitar, piano, organ, double bass, violin, recorder and most other instruments.

Written music is the same almost everywhere in the world. It is the same for most types of music, for singers and most instruments.

No matter what you play or sing, you will benefit from being able to read music.

You will be able to learn new pieces quickly and correctly. Thousands upon thousands of pieces of music are available for you to read and enjoy — music from all over the world — even from countries whose languages you don't understand. Almost any well-known piece of music can be bought from good music shops or borrowed from a library. It won't be necessary to learn each piece 'by heart' — you will be able to pick it up and read it whenever you wish.

You will also be sure that you are playing or singing each piece correctly — something which even the best of us are not always certain about when we 'play by ear'. You won't have to rely on someone else showing you how a piece should be played or sung — when you read music you will know for yourself. In a band, orchestra or choir, it is far better when everyone can read, instead of trying to remember what each should play or sing.

By reading music, you will be learning more and more about music and your playing or singing will become better and better. You will even find it easier to learn to play a new instrument.

Music is written as simply as it can be to tell us everything we need to know. Musical signs tell us which notes to play or sing, when and how they should be played or sung, and how long they should sound. Some of these signs may be new to you, but soon you will come to recognise them.

Music is written for everyone's enjoyment. You'll get the best out of it by learning to read it.

ROGER EVANS

How to use this book

Read everything slowly and carefully. Make sure you understand each section before going on to the next. If necessary, read the same pages several times until you know exactly what is meant.

Read each piece of music and look up anything which you may have forgotten. Most important, don't rush. Take your time learning how music works.

Do all this and, by the time you reach 'Choosing your first pieces of music' at the end of the first part of the book, you should be able to read most simple music.

The second part of the book explains certain things in more detail and deals with signs and words which are less frequently found in music. It isn't essential to learn all of these, but you should read about them so that you will understand and recognise them. Then, you can look them up if you come across them in written music.

The third part of the book is a Directory of Musical Signs and a Short Musical Dictionary. Both of these may be used as an index and for looking up musical signs and words. Please do not use them until you have read and completely understood all of the first part of the book, because they contain musical expressions which you may not yet know.

Some examples are given for the guitar, piano and organ. However, reading music is the same for other instruments, when you know the positions of the notes on them. A basic book about your instrument will give the positions of the notes if you don't already know them.

In this book, both the traditional and modern names for musical signs are given. For most purposes, it is not essential to learn the traditional names (which are shown in brackets everywhere except in the Dictionary.)

How Notes are named

Musical sounds, or NOTES as they are known, are named after the first seven letters of the alphabet:

$$A - B - C - D - E - F - G$$

After G, the note names start again at A:

$$A - B - C - D - E - F - G - \underline{A} - \underline{B} - \underline{C} \text{ and so on.}$$

1   2   3   4   5   6   7   8

As you can see, every eight notes there is another note with the same name. These notes are given the same names because they sound very much alike, in spite of being 'higher' or 'lower' than each other.

SOME NOTES ON THE KEYBOARD

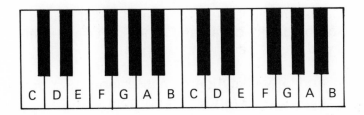

SOME NOTES ON THE GUITAR

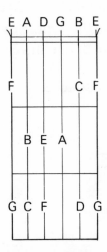

If you play an instrument, find out the names of the notes you play. (Look at a book about your instrument if necessary.) Then play two notes which have the same name and see how similar they sound.

How Notes are written

Written music is very versatile. It can show all the notes from the very highest sounds right down to the very lowest.

However, all notes are not needed for every instrument or voice. So, to simplify it, and make it easier to read, music is divided into two parts — one for higher voices and instruments, and one for lower.

Signs called CLEFS tell us whether a piece of music is for high or low instruments and voices. Two Clefs are normally used* and one or the other is shown at the beginning of every line of music.

THE TREBLE OR G CLEF (&)

Music with this Clef is for the higher (Soprano and Alto) voices and instruments, the guitar and the right hand of the piano, organ and other keyboard instruments.

THE BASS OR F CLEF (9:)

Music with this Clef is for the lower (Tenor and Bass) voices and instruments, and the left hand of the piano, organ and other keyboard instruments. It is also used for notes played on the pedals of an organ.

The piano, organ and other keyboard instruments use both Clefs together because they have such a wide range and number of notes.

Notes are written on sets of lines called STAVES. There is one Stave for the voices and instruments which use the Treble or G Clef (&) and another for the lower voices and instruments which use the Bass or F Clef (9:).

Each Stave has five lines and four spaces.

THE TREBLE CLEF AND STAVE

THE BASS CLEF AND STAVE

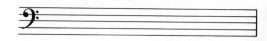

---

*There is also a third Clef, the C Clef (⅓). It is not generally used today except for the viola and sometimes for the higher notes of the 'cello, bassoon and tenor trombone. If your music is written with this Clef, turn to page 83 after you have read this section.

Each line and space on the Stave is like a step on a musical ladder — one note on the line, the next note higher in the space above, and so on. The higher the note sounds, the higher up it is on the Stave.

As long as you can remember the name of ONE note, you can work out all the others.

The Clefs help us by giving the position of one note. The Treble or G Clef gives us the position for the note G on the second line. The Clef draws a ring around the second line to show us.

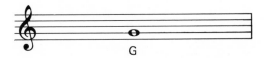

G

The other notes, higher and lower than G, run in order up and down the Stave. G is on the line, A is in the space above, B is on the next line, and so on.

HIGH NOTES AT TOP OF STAVE

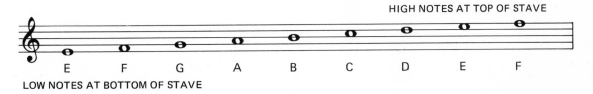

E   F   G   A   B   C   D   E   F

LOW NOTES AT BOTTOM OF STAVE

The Bass or F Clef also gives the position of one note — this time F on the fourth line. The big 'dot' of the Clef marks the note.

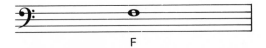

F

The other notes, higher and lower than F, run in order up and down the Stave. F on the line, G in the space above, and so on.

HIGH NOTES AT TOP OF STAVE

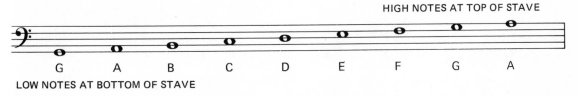

G   A   B   C   D   E   F   G   A

LOW NOTES AT BOTTOM OF STAVE

If you are a singer, or if the instrument you play only uses one Stave, it isn't essential to learn the notes on the other Stave. However, it is worthwhile to know how they both work.

WHERE THESE NOTES ARE ON THE KEYBOARD

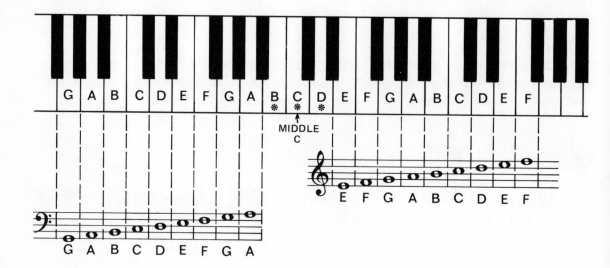

*THESE NOTES ARE EXPLAINED IN LATER PAGES.

. . . AND ON THE GUITAR

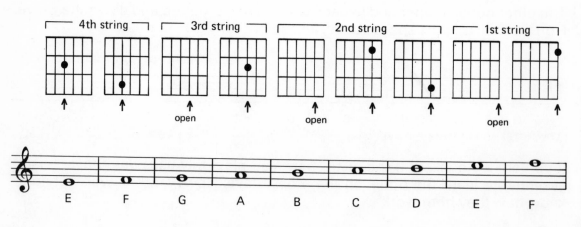

Here are some examples for you to practise reading notes. If you play an instrument, try playing the ones which are for your instrument. Treble and Alto instruments and the guitar should play the examples on the Treble or G Clef. Tenor and Bass instruments should play the examples on the Bass or F Clef. If you are not sure which you should use, look at a book about your instrument. The piano and organ should play both sets of examples — play the notes on the Bass Clef separately with the left hand.

Before you begin, make sure you know where the notes are on your instrument.

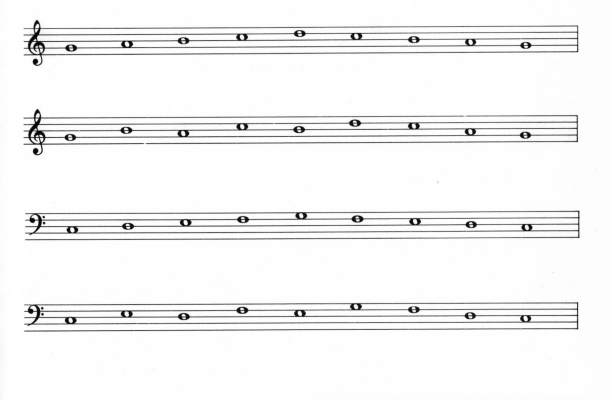

Note: Music for the guitar is written higher than it actually sounds so it can appear on the

Treble Clef (𝄞) and be easier to read. In guitar music ⟨E⟩ is the same note

as ⟨E⟩ on the piano, organ and other instruments.

Music for Tenor singers is sometimes written in this way on the Treble Clef. Some other instruments have their music written higher or lower than it sounds for similar reasons.

Notes with different shapes

As well as showing us which notes to play or sing, written music also tells us how long each note should sound — by giving notes different shapes.

So, the *position* of the note tells us *which note* to play or sing, the *shape* of the note tells us *how long it should sound*.

Each different shape lasts for a certain number of 'beats' which we can count.

o is a WHOLE NOTE (or SEMIBREVE). In most music it lasts for four beats. For this note we count 1—2—3—4—, in time with the music.

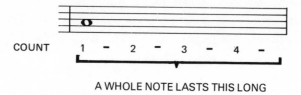

A WHOLE NOTE LASTS THIS LONG

♩ is a HALF NOTE (or MINIM). It usually lasts for two beats — half as long as a Whole Note. Count Half Notes like this:

EACH HALF NOTE LASTS
THIS LONG

♩ is a QUARTER NOTE (or CROTCHET) — a quarter of a Whole Note. It usually lasts for one beat. Count Quarter Notes like this:

EACH QUARTER NOTE
LASTS THIS LONG

♪ is an EIGHTH NOTE (or QUAVER). An Eighth Note usually lasts for half a beat. Two or more Eighth Notes may be joined together — ♫ . Count Eighth Notes one-and-two-and-

EACH EIGHTH NOTE
LASTS THIS LONG

14

The 'stems' of notes can go up (♩) or down (♩) — it doesn't make *any* difference to the note. Normally, to keep music tidy and clear, notes above the middle line of the Stave have their 'stems' pointing down. On the middle line they can go either way:

To make reading and counting easier, music is divided with vertical lines called BAR-LINES. The beat does not stop at Bar-Lines. Count evenly as if they don't exist — 1 — 2 — 3 — 4 — 1 — 2 — 3 — 4 — and so on. It will probably help if you tap your foot in time with the beat when you are counting.

The space, or measure between two Bar-Lines is called a BAR.

Bar-Lines also help to show the rhythm — the first note after a Bar-Line is normally played or sung a little more strongly than the others.

The end of a piece of music is always marked with a DOUBLE BAR-LINE. Double Bar-Lines also can divide music into sections or Phrases.

Try playing or humming this example, counting evenly in your head at the same time. If you like, tap your foot in time with the beats which are underlined. As you can see, there are four beats to the Bar.

Notes of different lengths may be mixed together in a Bar. The beats carry on regardless of the number, or length of notes.

Try playing or humming this, counting at the same time.

Reading a Melody

The first part of the theme of ODE TO JOY by Beethoven will give you some practice in reading and show you just how easy it is.

Read the notes first of all and make sure you know what they are. If necessary look them up. However, if I tell you that the first note is B, you should be able to work them out for yourself. Then work out the timing.

Notice how the first three bars of each line are exactly the same. Always look for phrases like these which repeat in music — it will make reading much easier.

Now, the same melody written on the Bass Clef. The timing is written in, so you can see if you worked it out correctly.

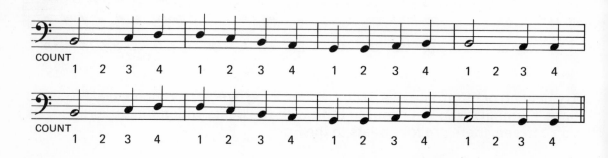

Music which is well written should give you an idea of the timing by the way the notes are spaced in each bar. However, the only way to get your timing completely right is to count out the notes in each bar until you know how they should sound. This is much easier, of course, when you already know a tune.

Sometimes it helps to write the timing underneath the notes. If you write on music, use a soft pencil and write lightly, so it can be rubbed out later.

Notes above and below the Staves

Most instruments and voices have more notes than can be shown on the five lines and four spaces of the Staves. These other notes are written in the spaces above and below each Stave, and on short lines called LEGER LINES.

These notes can be worked out in exactly the same way as the notes you have already seen — if F is on the line, G will be in the space above, A is on the next line, and so on.

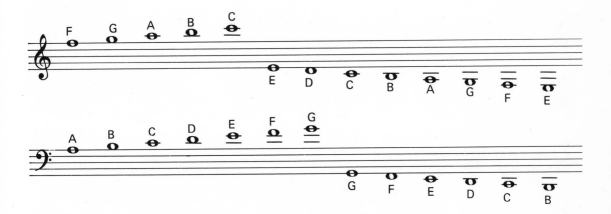

After a while you will come to recognise these notes. If you have any doubts, look them up or work them out for yourself.

Some notes overlap and appear on both Staves. This is particularly important for players of keyboard instruments which use both Staves. For most other people, these overlapping notes are of less interest. However, knowing how the Staves relate to one another will help you to understand music for other instruments and voices.

The note called 'Middle C' (roughly in the middle of the piano), is on the first Leger Line *below* the Treble Stave — *and* on the first Leger Line *above* the Bass Stave. It is shown here with some other notes which overlap:

The next piece of music is a French folk song called AU CLAIR DE LA LUNE. Read it, and it will help you learn to recognise notes on Leger Lines. You can look up the notes on the facing page, if you need to. Use the notes shown under the Keyboard, unless you play the guitar.

Notice that the first, second and fourth lines are exactly the same in this tune.

Now, the same tune written on the Bass Stave.

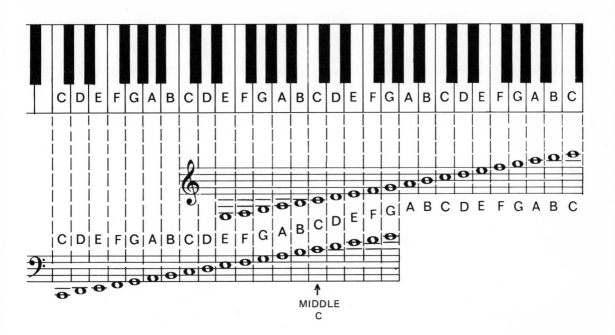

MIDDLE
C

NOTES ON THE GUITAR UP TO THE THIRD FRET

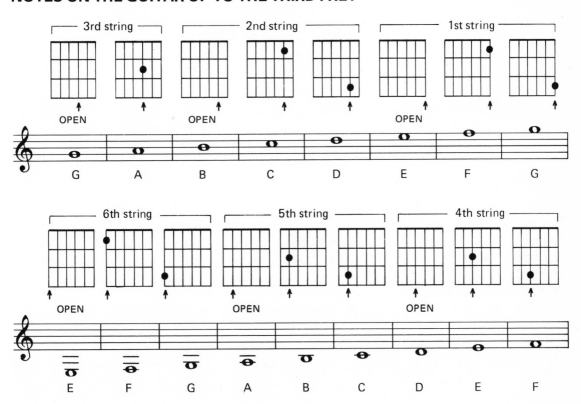

Rests

In many pieces of music, one or more of the players or singers is silent for a few beats. These silent beats are known as RESTS.

Rests may be found at the beginning of music — or at the end. Rests sometimes occur between the different 'Phrases' of a melody. In songs, you may find Rests which allow the singer to take a breath.

Rests are counted in exactly the same way as the notes which they replace.

NOTE   REST

o = This is a WHOLE NOTE (or SEMIBREVE) REST.
It lasts as long as a Whole Note — usually four beats.
Count 1 — 2 — 3 — 4 —.
Notice how it hangs from the line on the Stave.
The Whole Note Rest can also show a whole bar of silence.

♩ = HALF NOTE (or MINIM) REST.
This one sits on the line. It lasts as long as a Half Note — usually two beats. Count 1 — 2 —.

♩ = QUARTER NOTE (or CROTCHET) REST.
It lasts as long as a Quarter Note — usually one beat.

♪ = EIGHTH NOTE (or QUAVER) REST.
It lasts as long as an Eighth Note — usually half a beat.
(It looks a little like an Eighth Note which is lying down 'resting'.)

The timing of Rests is usually obvious from the way in which they, and the notes, are written — but you should count them to be sure. More than one Rest may appear in a bar, as you can see in the examples below. Try playing or humming these examples, counting to yourself at the same time. Count Rests as if they were notes.

1   2   3   4   1   2   3 & 4   1   2   3   4   1   2   3   4

Curved Lines

Sometimes a note carries on into the next bar. When this is to happen, a curved line called a TIE is used. This makes the first note longer by joining it to the note at the beginning of the next bar:

THE NOTE LASTS THIS LONG

Ties can also join two or more notes together in the same bar. This makes the first note last for the combined number of beats of notes 'tied' together:

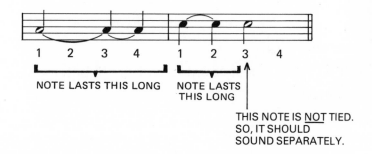

NOTE LASTS THIS LONG   NOTE LASTS THIS LONG

THIS NOTE IS <u>NOT</u> TIED. SO, IT SHOULD SOUND SEPARATELY.

Notice how a *separate* curved line links each note to the next.

Ties only work with notes which have the same name and same position on the Stave — and no different notes in between. The next example is NOT a Tie.

PLAY OR SING THESE NOTES SMOOTHLY

The curved line here has another meaning. Over or under several different notes, the curved line tells us that these notes should be played or sung smoothly. This curved line is called a SLUR.

Slurs also mark musical phrases, 'bowing' for stringed instruments like the violin, and the way words fit into songs. You will find 'Slurs' in most music.

Dotted Notes

A small 'dot' after any note makes it last half as long again (one and a half times its normal length.)

A Half Note (𝅗𝅥) which usually lasts for two beats, lasts for three beats with a dot after it (𝅗𝅥.).

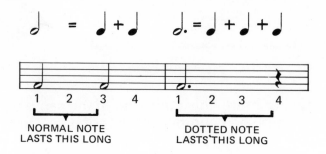

A Quarter Note (♩) which usually lasts for one beat, lasts for one and a half beats with a dot after it (♩.).

Dotted Quarter Notes are best counted with 'and' between each beat. You will often find them mixed with Eighth Notes (♪).

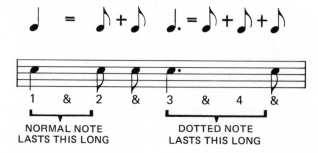

Dots work in the same way after Rests.

In a few pieces of Classical music, you may come across notes with more than one dot written after them. When this happens, each dot adds half as much again as the previous dot —

$$𝅗𝅥.. = ♩ + ♩ + ♩ + ♪$$

You have now covered quite a lot of musical ground and should already know how to read some music. Before continuing, go back and make sure you understand everything so far. Then try reading the next tune.

SILENT NIGHT, another tune for you to read, has some Dotted Notes, Rests and even a Tied Note at the end. Read and count these notes carefully.
The tune has three beats to the bar, count them 1— 2— 3   1— 2— 3. The timing of the notes and beats is written in to help you.

Time Signatures

At the beginning of all music you will find two numbers or a sign like a large letter 'C'. These are TIME SIGNATURES. They tell us how many beats there are in each bar, and the type (or value) of the beats.

Most Time Signatures consist of two numbers.

The top number tells us how many beats there are in each bar.

NUMBER OF BEATS ➞
TYPE (VALUE) OF BEATS ➞

The bottom number gives the type of beat:

2 for Half Notes (♩)

4 for Quarter Notes (♩)

8 for Eighth Notes (♪), and so on.

In the $\frac{2}{4}$ Time Signature shown above, the top number tells us there are two beats in the bar. The bottom number tells us that these beats are Quarter Notes. So, in $\frac{2}{4}$ music, there are two Quarter Note *beats* in each bar.

Except for 'Silent Night', all the music you have read up to this point in the book has been in $\frac{4}{4}$ Time. It has all had four Quarter Note *beats* in each bar.

NUMBER OF BEATS (4) ➞
TYPE OF BEATS ➞
($\overline{4}$ = QUARTER NOTES)

$\frac{4}{4}$ TIME is also often written with the sign '**C**'

4 Quarter = Note beats to the bar.

When speaking of Time Signatures, we usually say 'FOUR-FOUR' meaning $\frac{4}{4}$, 'TWO-FOUR' meaning $\frac{2}{4}$, and so on.

VERY IMPORTANT! The Time Signature refers to the number of BEATS — NOT the number of NOTES in each bar. Notes and rests of any lengths may be mixed together in a bar of music, as long as they add up to the number of beats shown by the Time Signature.

Here are some of the ways you may find notes and rests mixed together in bars of music in $\frac{4}{4}$ Time, and the way they are counted.

The Time Signature also tells us something else — the rhythm of the music. In all music, some beats are stronger than others. If this were not so, music would be very dull and uninteresting. The first beat in each bar is normally a little stronger than the others. In music with two beats to the bar, this gives a strong — weak, strong — weak, rhythm.

Try counting this out loud, tapping your foot at the same time, to get the feeling of two beats to the bar.

In music with four beats to the bar, the third beat is also stronger, but not as strong as the first beat. Try counting strong — weak — medium — weak, strong — weak — medium — weak.

$\frac{3}{4}$ or WALTZ TIME is the next most popular Time after $\frac{4}{4}$. As you can see from the Time Signature, there are three Quarter Note beats to the bar. The first beat in each bar should be stronger. The next two beats are weak. This gives a very distinctive rhythm — *One* — two — three, *Strong* — weak — weak. Try counting it.

Listen to some music and see if you can hear the different strengths of beats. When you have done this, go back over the tunes in the book and try them again, this time giving extra strength to notes which fall on strong and medium beats. Before you start to read, count out the beats and tap your foot at the same time. This will help you to get into the feeling of the rhythm. The first two tunes are in $\frac{4}{4}$, 'Silent Night' is in $\frac{3}{4}$.

CRADLE SONG by Brahms, the next tune, is also in $\frac{3}{4}$ Time, as you can see.

The first bar of a piece of music doesn't always have the number of beats you would expect from the Time Signature, The tune may start in the middle, or at the end of the first bar. When this happens, you should count the missing beats:

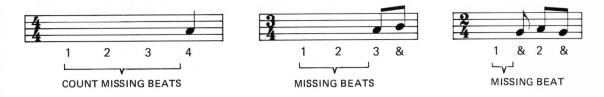

The beats which have been missed out are usually to be found in the last bar of the music — so everything finally adds up correctly.

WILDWOOD FLOWER is an American folk tune in $\frac{2}{4}$ time. It starts on the second beat of the first bar, as you can see.

Sharps, Flats and Naturals

So far, the music in this book has been written with the 'Natural' notes — A, B, C, D, E, F and G.

There are also some other notes which can be sung and played on most instruments. These other notes are called SHARPS and FLATS, and they are to be found between most of the 'Natural' notes.

The Sharp and Flat notes really stand out on the keyboard of the piano and organ, so first of all we will look at them there.

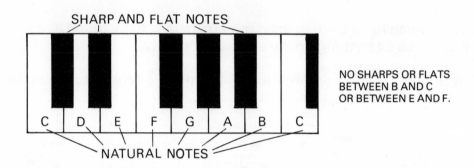

As you can see, there are no Sharps or Flats between B and C or between E and F, but there are Sharps and Flats between all the other notes. This applies to written music for all voices and instruments.

SHARPS (♯)

Sharp notes are marked by a Sharp sign — ♯

A Sharp note is higher than the Natural note with the same letter name —

The Sharp note above A is called 'A Sharp' — written A♯. This is the note between A and B.

The Sharp note above C is called C Sharp — written C♯. This is the note between C and D.

The Sharp above F is F Sharp (F♯), the Sharp above G is G Sharp (G♯), and so on . . .

NO SHARP NOTE HERE   NO SHARP NOTE HERE

A — A♯ -B ↓ C — C♯ — D — D♯ — E ↓ F — F♯ — G — G♯ — A

On the keyboard, a Sharp note is played on the black key above the Natural note with the same letter name:

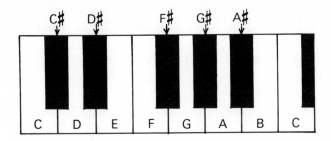

On the guitar and most 'fretted' instruments, a Sharp note is one fret higher than the Natural note with the same letter name:

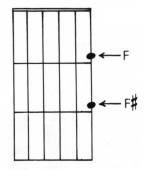

If you play another instrument, find the positions of the Sharp notes on it. If necessary look them up in an instruction book.

On the Staves, Sharp notes are shown by a Sharp sign (♯) in front of the note which is to be 'sharpened'.

FLATS (♭)

Flat notes are marked by a Flat sign — ♭

A Flat note is *lower* than the Natural note with the same letter name —

The Flat note *below* A is called 'A Flat' — written A♭. This is the note between A and G.

The Flat note below G is G Flat (G♭). This is the note between G and F.

The Flat below E is E Flat (E♭), the Flat below D is D Flat (D♭) and so on.

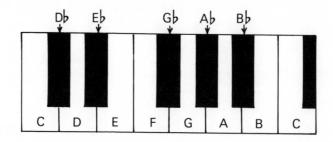

NO FLAT NOTE HERE   NO FLAT NOTE HERE

A – A♭ – G – G♭ – F – E – E♭ – D – D♭ – C – B – B♭ – A

On the keyboard, a Flat note is played on the black key below the Natural note with the same letter name:

D♭   E♭   G♭   A♭   B♭

C | D | E | F | G | A | B | C

On the guitar and most fretted instruments, a Flat note is one fret lower than the Natural note with the same letter name:

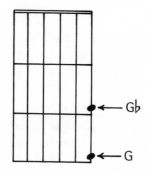

— G♭

— G

If you play another instrument, find the positions of the Flat notes on it. If necessary, look them up in an instruction book.

On the Staves, Flat notes are marked with a Flat sign ($\flat$) in front of the note which is to be 'flattened'.

For most playing and singing, each of these notes can be thought of as having a Flat and a Sharp name. A♯ is the same note as B♭, and so on.

A♯=B♭   C♯=D♭   D♯=E♭   F♯=G♭   G♯=A♭

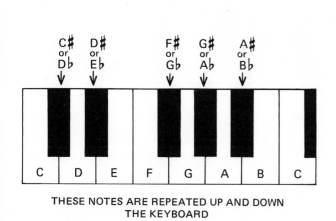

THESE NOTES ARE REPEATED UP AND DOWN
THE KEYBOARD

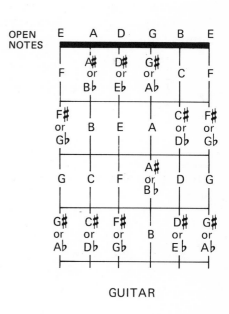

GUITAR

Notes are given different names for a good reason — sometimes it is easier to read and write music with Sharps, at other times it is easier with Flats.

As well as changing the notes which are marked by them, Sharp and Flat signs also affect all notes in the same position on the Stave which follow in the bar:

Sometimes the sign is repeated in brackets later in the bar as a reminder.

If the note is to be Sharp or Flat in the *next* bar, the sign is used again.

NATURAL SIGNS

A Sharp or Flat sign can be cancelled by a NATURAL SIGN (♮). Written in front of a note, it tells us that the Natural note is needed instead of a Sharp or Flat which was marked earlier. This sign also affects notes in the same position which follow in the same bar.

Another Sharp or Flat sign is used if the note is to be 'sharpened' or 'flattened' again.

Take care to read Sharps, Flats and Naturals correctly — otherwise your music will not sound right. If you have any doubts about Sharps, Flats or Naturals now, or in the future, read these pages again.

COVENTRY CAROL — a tune which has some Sharps. Look up the notes, if you need to, on pages 92-94. Remember to make the 'Tied Notes' last for the combined number of beats of the notes 'tied' by the curved lines.

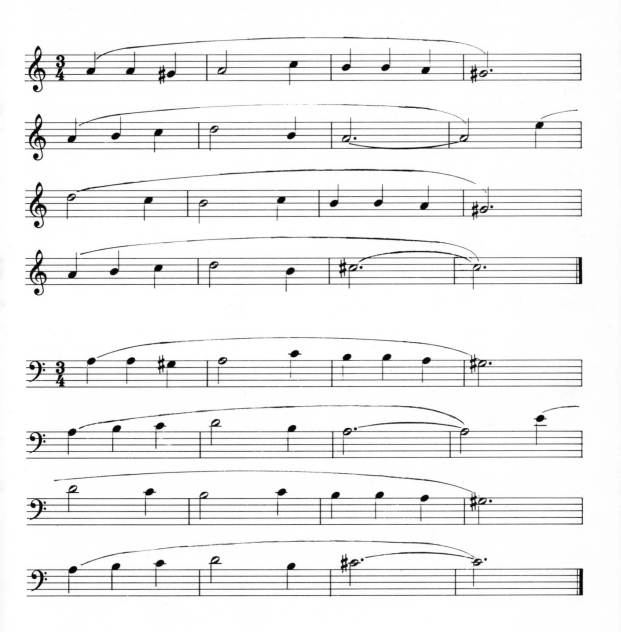

Keys and Key Signatures

As you have seen in previous pages, Sharps, Flats and Naturals may be written into music when they are needed. These extra 'written in' Sharps, Flats and Naturals are called ACCIDENTALS.

However, Sharps and Flats are often so much a part of the music that they are shown right at the beginning, immediately after the Clef. These Sharp and Flat signs at the beginning of music make up what are known as KEY SIGNATURES.

The Sharp or Flat signs of Key Signatures are written in the positions of the notes to be affected. ALL NOTES with the same name as the ones marked are changed, from the beginning to the end of the music.

Here the Sharp signs are in the position of the note F (shown in brackets). This means *every* F must be sharpened:

EVERY F IS SHARPENED WHEN F♯ IS IN THE KEY SIGNATURE

Key Signatures are repeated after the Clef on every line of music as a reminder.

Unless extra 'Accidental' Sharp, Flat or Natural signs are written in, we know the names of the notes we may expect to find in music with this Key Signature — All the notes except F♯ will be Natural notes:

G—A—B—C—D—E—F♯—G

There is no F, of course, because the Key Signature changed it to F Sharp.

34

These notes in alphabetical order starting with G make up what is known as a SCALE. Scales are named after the starting note or KEY NOTE, so this is the Scale for the Key of G. (The full name is G MAJOR.)
It can start on any G. Play it, if you like, and see how familiar it sounds. Music in the Key of G Major is based upon the notes named in this Scale. The Key of G Major has one Sharp in the Key Signature.

Some people find it helpful to play or sing the Scale of the Key of a piece of music before starting to read it. They do this to get the feeling of the Key, and to know which notes to expect. For this reason, the notes of the Scale are shown here under each Key Signature.

SOME KEY SIGNATURES

ONE SHARP — THE KEY OF G   (G Major)
The Key Signature with one Sharp sharpens *every F*

   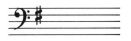   EVERY F TO BE SHARPENED

In music with this Key Signature we would expect these notes:

G A B C D E F♯ G   (The Scale of G Major)

TWO SHARPS — THE KEY OF D   (D Major)
The Key Signature with two Sharps sharpens *every F and every C*

      EVERY F AND EVERY C
                                                               TO BE SHARPENED

In music with this Key Signature we would expect these notes:

D E F♯ G A B C♯ D   (The Scale of D Major)

THREE SHARPS — THE KEY OF A   (A Major)

In music with this Key Signature we would expect these notes:

A B C♯ D E F♯ G♯ A   (The Scale of A Major)

The Sharp signs of Key Signatures always follow this pattern:

One Sharp is always F♯
Two Sharps are always F♯ and C♯
Three Sharps are always F♯, C♯ and G♯

Flat Key Signatures are written in a similar way.

ONE FLAT — THE KEY OF F   (F Major)

EVERY B TO BE FLATTENED

The Flat sign (♭) is in the position of the note B (shown in brackets). This means *every* B must be flattened.

In music with this Key Signature we would expect these notes:

F G A B♭ C D E F   (The Scale of F Major)

TWO FLATS — THE KEY OF B FLAT (B♭ Major)

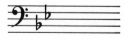

EVERY B AND EVERY E TO BE FLATTENED

In music with this Key Signature we would expect these notes:

B♭ C D E♭ F G A B♭   (The Scale of B♭ Major)

36

THREE FLATS — THE KEY OF E FLAT   (E♭ Major)

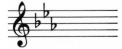   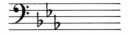

EVERY B, EVERY E
AND EVERY A TO BE
FLATTENED

In music with this Key Signature we would expect these notes:

E♭ F G A♭ B♭ C D E♭   (The Scale of E♭ Major)

Another Key Signature has already appeared in this book — the Key Signature with no Sharps or Flats.

NO SHARPS OR FLATS — THE KEY OF C   (C Major)

   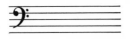

ALL NATURAL NOTES

With this Key Signature we would expect all the natural notes:

C D E F G A B C   (The Scale of C Major)

As well as the Sharps or Flats of the Key Signature, you may find extra 'Accidental' Sharp, Flat or Natural signs written in to music in any Key.

Occasionally, a piece of music 'changes Key' in the middle. When this is to happen, a Double Bar-Line and a new Key Signature is shown where the change is to take place. Any Sharps or Flats which are not needed from the first Key Signature are cancelled by Natural signs:

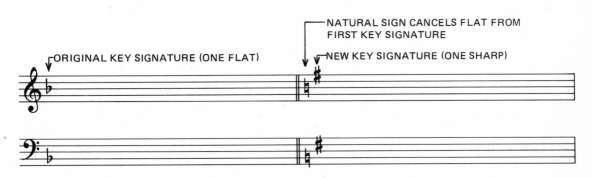

Music is written in different Keys to make it more interesting for both the performer and the listener. It would be very boring for everyone if the same notes were used all the time. If you perform for other people, it is a good idea to choose music in different Keys, and at different speeds, so that no piece will sound like the one before.

Different Keys allow music to be played or sung by different instruments and voices. A tune in one Key may be too high or too low for you, but just right in another Key. Sometimes music is too difficult for an instrument in one Key, so it is 're-arranged' in another easier Key.

Music is also written in different Keys for other reasons. Some instruments sound better when played in certain Keys, so music for them is usually in these Keys. Pieces of music may be written in a particular Key because that Key best suits the feeling of the music.

Before you start to read a piece of music, look at the Key Signature and it will tell you which notes to expect.

If you have any doubts about Key Signatures, refer to these pages and this rule:

The Sharp or Flat signs in a Key Signature are written after the Clef in the position of one note only, but ALL NOTES OF THE SAME NAME in the music must be sharpened or flattened. The only exceptions to this happen where extra 'Accidental' Sharp, Flat or Natural signs are written in, or if a new Key Signature occurs.

The next two pieces of music will help you to learn to read music with Sharp or Flat Key Signatures.

RED RIVER VALLEY, an American folk song.
The Key Signature is for the key of F which has one Flat — B♭. (Every B will be flattened.) We can therefore expect to find some or all of these notes: F G A B♭ C D E F. To help you, the Flats are marked with a small asterisk (*). Look up the notes, if you need to, on pages 92-94. The Time Signature tells us that there are four quarter note beats to the bar.

Theme from JESU JOY OF MAN'S DESIRING by J. S. Bach.
The Key Signature is for the Key of G which has one Sharp — F♯. (Every F will be sharpened.) We can therefore expect to find some or all of these notes: G A B C D E F♯. To help you, the Sharps are marked with a small asterisk (*). Look up the notes, if you need to, on pages 92-94. The Time Signature tells us there are three quarter note beats to the bar.

How Fast?

So far, all the music in this book could have been played or sung quickly or slowly depending on how the beats were counted, and how you felt about it. Music is, of course, a matter of personal taste, and the way it is performed depends very much on the player, singer or leader of a band or orchestra. However, the composer or writer of music usually gives an idea of how he or she feels it should be performed.

An indication of the speed of the music (or TEMPO, as it is known), is normally given at the beginning of the music in English or Italian. Italian has been the international language of music for many years, but today English is normally found in modern music. The words do not refer to a definite speed, but give an idea of how fast the music is meant to be. The 'feeling' of the music is also sometimes suggested.

English words such as these have fairly obvious meanings, when used to describe a piece of music:

Very Slowly	March Time	Lively
Slow	Moderate (medium)	Rather Fast
Steady	Brightly	Very Fast

The title of music or the words of a song often gives an idea of how it should be played or sung. 'Cradle Song' would be performed 'Gently and Slowly', for example. Other music in this book could be described like this:

'Ode to Joy' — *Joyfully, Brightly.*

'Silent Night' — *Slowly and sweetly.*
'Coventry Carol' — *Slowly.*
'Jesu Joy of Man's Desiring' —*Brightly.*

'Au Clair de la Lune' — *Steady, moderate.*
'Wildwood Flower' — *Medium tempo.*
'Red River Valley' — *Moderately.*

Here are some of the more common Italian words used for Tempo, from the slowest to the fastest:

Lento or Largo	= Very Slow
Adagio	= Slow, Leisurely
Andante	= At 'walking pace'
Moderato (Mod.)	= Medium
Allegro	= Fast, Merry
Vivace	= Lively
Presto	= Very Fast
Molto	= Very (Molto Allegro = Very Fast)

Music sometimes changes speed to match a change of mood, or to create a dramatic effect. The following words and signs are written where the change is to take place:

Rallentando (Rall.) ⎫
Ritardando (Ritard.)⎬ Slow down gradually

Accelerando (Accel.) = Speed up gradually.

A Tempo = Go back to original speed

⌢ This is a PAUSE or HOLD SIGN. Written over a note or rest, it tells us that the note or rest is to last for more than its normal length. The actual length is left for the player or singer to decide. It is often found at the end of a piece of music.

THE PAUSE OR HOLD SIGN OVER A NOTE OR REST MAKES IT LAST LONGER

The sign is also used where there is to be a pause in music.

Other words which are used for Tempo or feeling may be found in the Short Musical Dictionary which starts on page 95, in a full dictionary of music, or even in an Italian dictionary! Occasionally, you may come across foreign words in music from other countries. Where the meaning is not obvious, look them up in a dictionary of the language of the country.

More accurate Tempos are sometimes given in Classical music. A note sign and a number tell how many beats of that type (or value) there are to be to a minute.

For example, ♩ = 78 means there should be seventy-eight quarter note beats in a minute. This allows us to guess the speed, or use a clockwork instrument called a 'metronome' which can be set to tick at the speed required.

How Loud?

Music should have different levels of volume — loudness — depending on its feeling or mood. 'Silent Night' would naturally be played or sung fairly softly, but not all music is as obvious.

To help us decide, the writer of the music often gives an idea of how loud or soft a piece should be. A sign or word — usually in Italian — is written below the Stave at the beginning of the piece to tell us how loudly it should start. If the volume is to change in the middle of the music, another sign or word is written where the change is to take place.

SIGN	NAME	MEANING
ppp	Pianississimo	As softly as possible
pp	Pianissimo	Very softly
p	Piano	Softly
mp	Mezzo-Piano	Moderately softly
m	Mezzo	Medium, (mezzo means 'half')
mf	Mezzo-Forte	Moderately loudly
f	Forte	Loudly
ff	Fortissimo	Very loudly
fff	Fortississimo	As loudly as possible
pf	Più forte	More loudly
fp	Fortepiano	A sudden change from loud to soft
cres. or $<$	Crescendo	Gradually become louder
dim. or $>$	Diminuendo	Gradually become softer

Musical Shorthand

ABBREVIATION SIGNS — a sort of musical shorthand — are often found in music which is to be played or sung more than once. The signs are mainly used to save space but, when written clearly, they also make music easier to read. You will often come across them in music, so you should be able to recognise them and know how they work.

Most important is the REPEAT SIGN — a Double Bar with two dots:

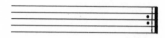

This sign tells us to return to a similar sign facing the other way around *or* if there is no other sign, go back to the beginning. The music in between is then repeated.

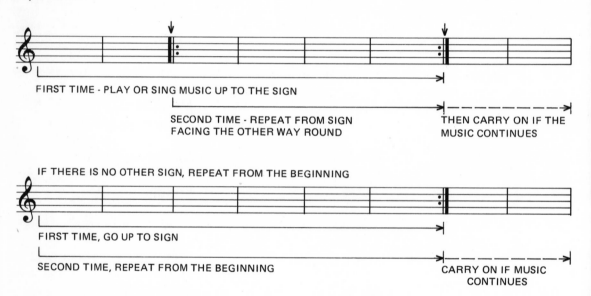

FIRST TIME - PLAY OR SING MUSIC UP TO THE SIGN

SECOND TIME - REPEAT FROM SIGN FACING THE OTHER WAY ROUND

THEN CARRY ON IF THE MUSIC CONTINUES

IF THERE IS NO OTHER SIGN, REPEAT FROM THE BEGINNING

FIRST TIME, GO UP TO SIGN

SECOND TIME, REPEAT FROM THE BEGINNING

CARRY ON IF MUSIC CONTINUES

FIRST and SECOND TIME BARS
First time around, the music includes the Bar marked 1   . Second time around, this Bar is left out and replaced by the music marked 2

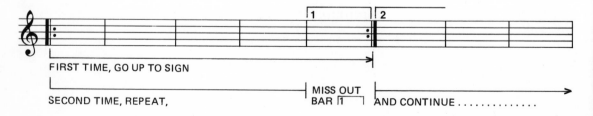

FIRST TIME, GO UP TO SIGN

SECOND TIME, REPEAT,

MISS OUT BAR 1   AND CONTINUE . . . .

44

Other signs are used in similar ways:

D.C. or *Da Capo* means repeat from the beginning.

D.S. or *Dal Segno* means 'Go back and repeat from this sign — 𝄋

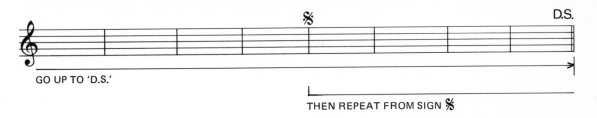

GO UP TO 'D.S.'

THEN REPEAT FROM SIGN 𝄋

Al Coda or 'To Coda' means 'go to the Coda'. The Coda (tail) is an extra few bars added to the end of the music. The Coda is marked by this sign: ⊕

D.S. al Coda means go back to the sign — 𝄋 — and repeat until you come to '*Al Coda* ⊕ '. Then go to the Coda, like this:

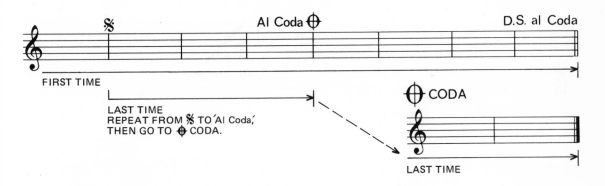

FIRST TIME

LAST TIME
REPEAT FROM 𝄋 TO 'Al Coda,'
THEN GO TO ⊕ CODA.

⊕ CODA

LAST TIME

The word FINE (finish) or the Pause Sign (⌒) over a Double Bar-Line often shows where the music is to end.

When you come across these signs, return to these pages and look them up. Work out the order of the music before you start to read it. In songs, the order is usually obvious if you look at the words.

Notes played or sung together

In most music several notes are played or sung at the same time. Often two or more musicians or singers play or sing different notes which blend together 'in harmony'. The piano, organ, guitar and other instruments can all play more than one note at a time.

When this is to happen, the notes which are to be played or sung together are written one above the other on the Staves:

NOTES WHICH ARE ONE ABOVE THE OTHER ARE PLAYED OR SUNG AT THE SAME TIME

When the notes have 'stems', the same stem may be used for both notes:

Music is normally written in this way when the notes last for the same time, and are for the same instrument.

When the notes are for two voices or instruments, one plays or sings the top line of notes and the other the bottom line. The stems of the notes on the top line then go up, and those on the bottom go down, making each Part easier to follow. (Music for a particular instrument or voice is called a 'Part')

TOP LINE OF NOTES: 1ST INSTRUMENT OR VOICE
BOTTOM LINE OF NOTES: 2ND INSTRUMENT OR VOICE.

If both instruments or voices have the same note, a stem is drawn top and bottom:

BOTH PLAY OR SING THE SAME NOTE

The top notes may be longer or shorter than the notes on the bottom — but you can see how they fit together by the way they are written.

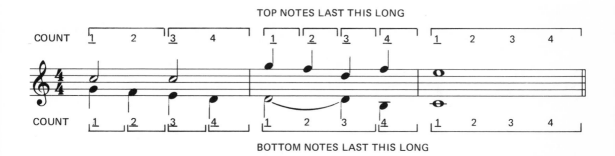

One 'Part' can have rests, while the other plays or sings. One may have long notes, while the other has short notes. Sometimes, they seem to be going their own separate ways, but they sound together when their notes are one above the other.

The two parts also share the same beats. If two or more people are playing or singing together, it is a good idea to count several beats before you start, so you will all keep in time. Make sure that notes which are one above the other sound at exactly the same time.

The top line of notes is usually the melody, which can be played or sung with or without the other lines of notes. If you are playing or singing on your own, this is the line which you would normally read. In fact, many musicians call the melody of a piece of music 'The Top Line'.

The other lines of notes are named after the voice or instrument for which they are written — the Bass Part, the Trumpet Part, and so on. The piano, organ and guitar often play two or more lines at the same time, but even with these it may help if you think of each line as a separate 'Part'.

Music with two or more lines of notes is also written in the same way on the Bass Stave:

Music on more than one Stave

Music is often written on two or more Staves, which are joined together by a line at the beginning and by Bar-Lines. Written this way, each voice or instrument can have its own separate Stave making it very clear and easy to follow.

1st INSTRUMENT OR VOICE

2nd INSTRUMENT OR VOICE

Music written on two Staves works in the same way as music on one Stave — Notes which are one above the other are played or sung at the same time; one Part may have longer or shorter notes or rests, and so on.

When two Staves are used for the same instrument — or for a group of instruments or voices — a large bracket called a BRACE joins them together:

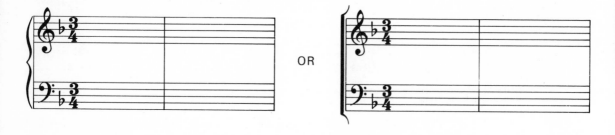

OR

Music for keyboard instruments is written this way. The Treble Stave is used for the right hand and the Bass Stave for the left. Each hand may play two or more notes at the same time, or one hand may play while the other holds a note or has a rest.

PIANO AND ORGAN

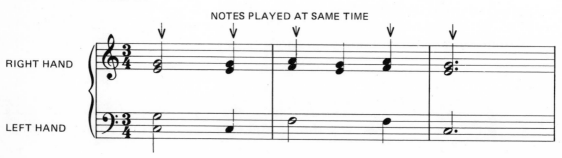

NOTES PLAYED AT SAME TIME

RIGHT HAND

LEFT HAND

48

If more Parts are to be played or sung at the same time, they may also be joined together. On the left, is the way most popular music is written. Organ music, on the right, often has a separate Stave for the pedals:

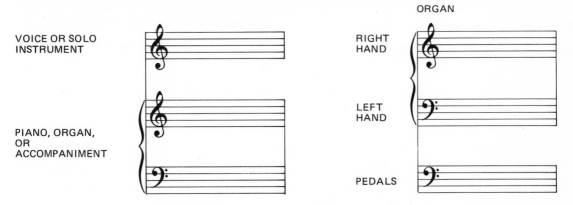

The Parts for all the instruments and voices needed in a piece of music are often shown together, one above the other, in what is known as a SCORE.

The Score for an orchestra or choir may have a separate Stave for each instrument or voice — this is a FULL SCORE. The Full Score usually has a large number of Staves and takes the whole of a page for just one line of music. To save space, the more convenient SHORT SCORE is often used instead. This gives the Parts for all voices or instruments on two Staves.

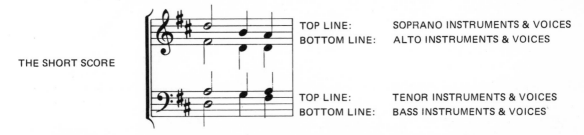

In a Full Orchestral Score, you may find music for some instruments written with what seem to be the wrong Key Signatures. These instruments — usually clarinets, trumpets and horns — have their music written in a different Key to which it sounds. Music for the B♭ clarinet, for example, written in the Key of C *sounds* in the Key of B Flat. B Flat is the real Key of the music and is the Key in which the piano and most other instruments would be playing.

Music for brass bands is also usually written in different Keys to which it sounds. The instruments which have music written in this way are called TRANSPOSING INSTRUMENTS.

Chords

The sound of two or more notes being played or sung together is called a CHORD.

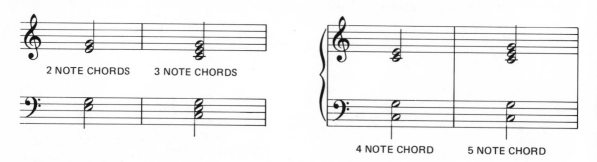

2 NOTE CHORDS   3 NOTE CHORDS

4 NOTE CHORD   5 NOTE CHORD

Chords can be played on the guitar, piano, organ and other instruments which are able to make more than one note at a time. Chords can also be made by two or more voices or instruments singing or playing together in harmony. Chords are found all the time in music — there were Chords in the previous two sections of this book.

Chords are named after their most important note. There are 'A Chords', 'B Chords', 'C Chords', 'B Flat Chords', 'C Sharp Chords' and so on. In fact, there are Chords for every Key. These Chord names are known as CHORD SYMBOLS.

Chord Symbols are often shown above or below the Stave. Most popular music also gives 'Chord Shapes' for the guitar, and occasionally Chord Shapes for the organ and piano.

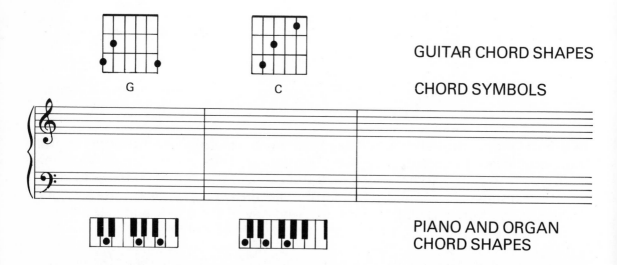

G   C

GUITAR CHORD SHAPES

CHORD SYMBOLS

PIANO AND ORGAN
CHORD SHAPES

Where there are no Chord Symbols, you can usually make the Chords by reading the notes on the Staves.

There are two basic kinds of Chords — MAJOR CHORDS and MINOR CHORDS. There is one note difference between them, but it changes the sound a lot. Major Chords sound bright and happy, Minor Chords sound a little sad. If you can, try these Chords on a piano, organ or guitar and hear the difference between them.

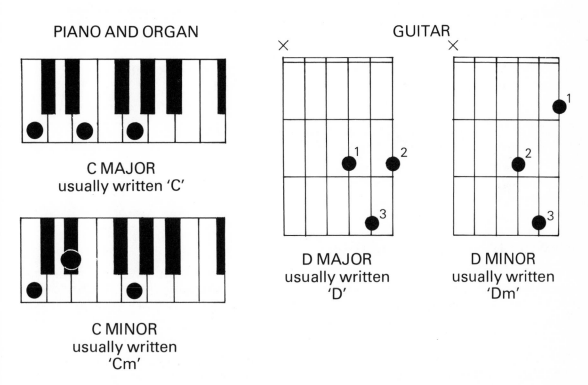

PIANO AND ORGAN

C MAJOR
usually written 'C'

C MINOR
usually written
'Cm'

GUITAR

D MAJOR
usually written
'D'

D MINOR
usually written
'Dm'

Major Chords are often known by the note name only — 'C Major' is usually written 'C'. Minor Chords are indicated with a small 'm' — 'Cm' is 'C Minor' and so on.

Chords sometimes have a number or word after the name — G7 (called G SEVEN), Dm6 (D Minor Six), C Aug. (C Augmented), for example. These Chords have extra notes added or have been changed in some way from the usual Major and Minor Chords.

Books of Chords for the piano, organ, guitar and other instruments are available from music shops, should you want one.

On the piano and organ you can often get a better effect by reading the notes on the Staves rather than using the Chord Symbols. A good book of Chords is essential, however, for most guitarists as the Chord Shapes shown on sheet music do not always give full Chords.

Chord Symbols are sometimes used on their own, for example in music for rhythm guitar. Instead of writing the Chord Symbol each time a Chord is to be played, strokes (**/**) tell us to *repeat* the Chord. Each stroke is for an *extra* beat.

EACH CHORD TO BE PLAYED FOUR TIMES   EACH CHORD TO BE PLAYED TWICE

The strokes are left out in some music, leaving us to work out the number of beats from the Time Signature:

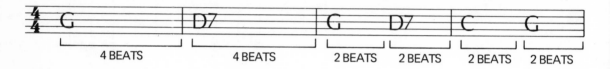

4 BEATS   4 BEATS   2 BEATS   2 BEATS   2 BEATS   2 BEATS

BROKEN CHORDS OR 'ARPEGGIOS'

An ARPEGGIO is a Chord with the notes sounded very quickly, one after the other — starting with the lowest note. The name 'Arpeggio' comes from the Italian word for 'harp', which gives a good idea of the effect. Arpeggios are shown by a sign ⦂ or (in front of the Chord.

On the guitar and keyboard, all the notes should continue after they have been sounded, so the full Chord is heard at the end of the Arpeggio.

An Arpeggio written —   Sounds roughly like this —

PLAY VERY QUICKLY

On other instruments — where only one note can be played at a time — the notes are simply sounded one after the other, very quickly.

52

Choosing your first pieces of music

If you have understood most of the book up to this point, you should now know how to read most music. You are probably keen to try a piece of your own choosing, but before you do, read on. Here are a few hints to help you choose, and make sure you don't attempt anything too difficult before you are ready.

First, choose tunes you know, or have heard and would recognise. Have several different pieces in mind, so you have a number of choices if one cannot be found, or is too difficult for you at the moment. You can buy music from most good music shops and borrow some pieces from certain libraries.

If possible get music which is 'arranged' for your instrument or voice. The shopkeeper may be able to recommend albums of several tunes which are better value than single pieces of music.

Take your time and look at the music before you buy it.

Make sure that it is written with the right Clef — 𝄞 or 𝄢 — for your instrument or voice.

Choose music which is not too long — or has too many notes. At first, avoid tunes which have a lot of Eighth Notes or dotted notes.

Try to find music which has no Sharps (♯) or Flats (♭). If this is not possible for tunes which you like, try pieces with no more than two Sharps or Flats in the Key Signature.

Choose simple Time Signatures — $\frac{2}{4}$ $\frac{3}{4}$ $\frac{4}{4}$ or 𝄴

Finally, choose music which is not too fast — medium and slow tunes are best at first.

When you have your music, find a quiet place to study it. Look at it closely and find out as much as possible about it, before you start to read it.

Look at the beginning. This always tells us a lot about a piece of music:

1 Are there Sharps or Flats in the Key Signature? How many of them are there?

Remember that these signs affect EVERY note with the same name as the one marked. If there is one Sharp, it will be F Sharp. EVERY F will become F Sharp, unless cancelled by a Natural Sign (♮). If you have any doubts about the way Key Signatures work, look back to pages 34-38.

2 What is the Time Signature?

$\frac{2}{4}$　is two quarter note beats to the bar and the rhythm should be _ONE_ — two, _ONE_ — two, and so on.

$\frac{3}{4}$　is three quarter note beats to the bar — _ONE_ — two — three, _ONE_ — two — three.

$\frac{4}{4}$　or **c** is four quarter note beats to the bar — _ONE_ — two — _three_ — four, _ONE_ — two — _three_ — four, and so on.

When you come to read the music, count the beat slowly and evenly until you understand the timing of all the notes. Look back to pages 14-15 or 20-22 if you are not sure about counting notes or rests, or pages 24-25 about Time Signatures.

3 How fast is the music?

Look up any words used for the Tempo in the Musical Dictionary at the back of the book, if the meaning isn't obvious.

4 How loud is the music? Look and see if it has loud and soft parts. The signs used for Volume are shown on page 43.

  1. KEY SIGNATURE. see pages 34-38

    3. TEMPO (SPEED). see Dictionary at back

Moderato

  4. VOLUME. see page 43

  2. TIME SIGNATURE. see pages 24-25

5 Look at all the notes in the music.
What are the highest and lowest notes? Can you play or sing them? Do you know where all the notes are on your instrument — including any Sharps or Flats in the music? If necessary, look up any notes on pages 92-94 or in a book about your instrument. Work out how to play or sing all the notes before worrying about their timing.

6 Look at any signs which are in the music.
Do you know what they mean? If not, look them up in previous pages or in the Directory of Musical Signs at the back of the book.

7 Try to see if any of the music is repeated. This may save you the trouble of working things out more than once. If Repeat signs are used, work out the order of the music before you start to read it. Repeat signs are shown on pages 44-45.

Now, you should know everything about this piece of music and be able to go ahead and read it with confidence. Get the feeling of it by humming the tune to yourself. Then, read it from the beginning to the end, stopping only to practise any parts which may be more difficult. If a few bars seem to slow you up each time you read the tune, practise these bars on their own until you can play or sing them as well as the rest.

The more you read, the better you will become. When you have read one piece of music, go on and try another. However, don't try music which is too difficult for you — even pieces you like very much. You will find it better to work up slowly, step by step to more complicated music. Remember, being able to play or sing a simple tune really well is far better than performing a difficult piece badly. If you play or sing to other people, keep to music which you are happy and confident to perform.

From here on the book deals with notes and signs which are not so common, but still important and likely to be found every so often. Read on so you will understand these things. If you come across any signs which you don't recognise or remember, look them up in the Directory of Musical Signs which starts on page 85. The Short Musical Dictionary, also at the end of the book, may be used as an index and for looking up any musical words you don't understand or remember. Look up any notes which you don't remember on pages 92-94.

Good luck with your music, may it give you a lot of enjoyment.

Other Notes and Rests

Sometimes, notes which are even shorter than Eighth Notes are used.

 or ♪ is a SIXTEENTH NOTE (or SEMIQUAVER). It lasts for half as long as an Eighth Note. Two or more Sixteenth Notes may be joined together:

They may also be joined to Eighth Notes and written:

AN EIGHTH NOTE ➜   ← 2 SIXTEENTH NOTES

When Sixteenth Notes are in groups, they can be counted like this:

<u>1</u> 2 3 4 <u>2</u> 2 3 4 <u>3</u> 2 3 4 <u>4</u> 2 3 4

Tap your foot in time with the beats which are underlined.

Sixteenth Notes may be mixed with other notes, and counted like this:

<u>1</u> 2 3 4 <u>2</u> 2 3 4 <u>1</u> 2 3 4 <u>2</u> 2 3 4

<u>1</u> <u>2</u> and <u>3</u> 2 3 4 <u>4</u> 2 3 4 <u>1</u> <u>2</u> 2 3 4 <u>3</u> <u>4</u> 2 3 4

Use these examples to help you work out the timing of Sixteenth Notes if you come across them.

Always start your counting slowly and evenly — you can get quicker when you know the rhythm of the notes.

Notes which are even shorter are not often found, but they are shown here to make the book as complete as possible.

♪ or ♪ is a THIRTY-SECOND NOTE (or DEMI-SEMIQUAVER).
It is half as long as a Sixteenth Note. If you come across these notes, count them like this: <u>1</u> & 2 & 3 & 4 & <u>2</u> & 2 & 3 & 4 &, and so on.

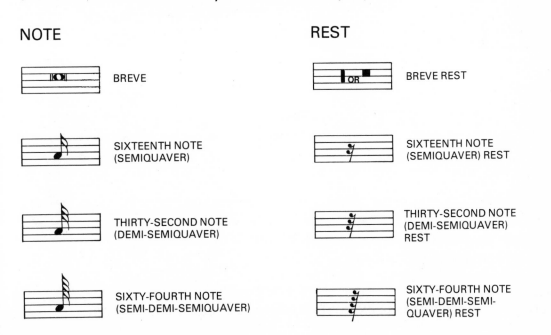

♪ or ♪ is a SIXTY-FOURTH NOTE (or SEMI-DEMI-SEMIQUAVER).
This is the shortest note which is very rarely used, even in Classical music. It is half as long as a Thirty-Second Note.

There is just one other note —

𝅝 This is the BREVE which is twice as long as a Whole Note. When a Whole Note lasts for four beats, the Breve lasts for eight beats. These days the Breve is not normally used except in Church music.

There are also Rests which have the same 'value' as all these notes, and which are counted in the same way as the notes they replace.

NOTE   REST

BREVE	BREVE REST
SIXTEENTH NOTE (SEMIQUAVER)	SIXTEENTH NOTE (SEMIQUAVER) REST
THIRTY-SECOND NOTE (DEMI-SEMIQUAVER)	THIRTY-SECOND NOTE (DEMI-SEMIQUAVER) REST
SIXTY-FOURTH NOTE (SEMI-DEMI-SEMIQUAVER)	SIXTY-FOURTH NOTE (SEMI-DEMI-SEMIQUAVER) REST

Triplets

In some music, three notes may be fitted into the time of two. When this is to happen, the notes are grouped together with a curved line and the figure '3'. This is called a TRIPLET.

Each note of the Triplet must be given the same length as the others. The secret to understanding them is found by counting slowly and evenly until you know the rhythm.

Count the beats in your head or out loud at the same time. Tap your foot only on the beats which are underlined.

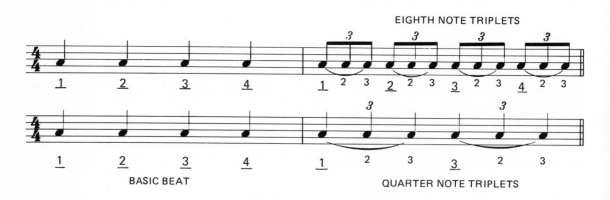

Of course, Triplets may be mixed with other notes:

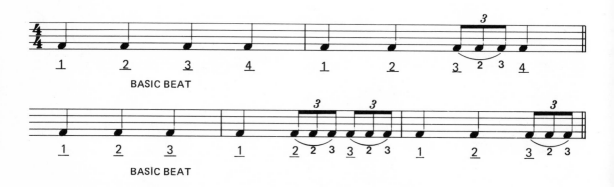

Try counting out all of these examples before you read the next tune.

58

AMAZING GRACE is a tune with Triplets. The timing of the notes is shown to help you to read it.

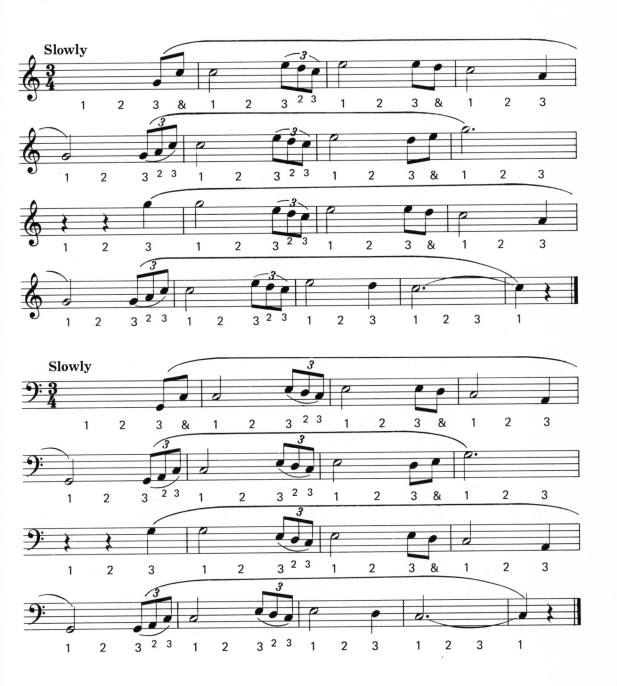

59

More Time Signatures

As explained earlier in the book, Time Signatures are written at the beginning of music to tell us how many beats there are to be in each bar, and the type or 'value' of each beat.

The top number of the Time Signature tells us how many beats. The bottom number tells us the type of beats:

$\overline{2}$ for Half Notes ($\flat$), $\overline{4}$ for Quarter Notes ($\flat$), $\overline{8}$ for Eighth Notes ($\flat$)) and $\overline{16}$ for Sixteenth Notes ($\flat$)).

$\frac{4}{4}$ may also be written $\mathbf{C}$, meaning four Quarter Notes beats to the bar.

$\frac{2}{2}$ may also be written $\mathbf{\phi}$, meaning two Half Notes beats to the bar.

The Time Signature refers to the number of beats and not to the number of notes in each bar. Any number of notes and rests may be mixed together in a bar, but they should add up to the number of beats of the Time Signature.

As you have already seen, the Time Signature does not set the speed of the music. However, fast music is not likely to be written in Half Note Time Signatures, such as $\frac{3}{2}$ — nor is slow music likely to be written in Eighth Note Time Signatures, such as $\frac{3}{8}$

Most, but not all of these things were explained earlier. They have been repeated here as a reminder before we go on to look at other Time Signatures.

With all Time Signatures, the first beat in the bar is the strongest beat:

2 BEATS TO THE BAR

1	2
STRONG	WEAK

1	2
STRONG	WEAK

1	2
STRONG	WEAK

$\mathbf{\phi}$ OR $\frac{2}{2}$ = 2 HALF NOTE BEATS TO THE BAR

$\frac{2}{4}$ = 2 QUARTER NOTE BEATS TO THE BAR

$\frac{2}{8}$ = 2 EIGHTH NOTE BEATS TO THE BAR

Notice how the *rhythm* in each bar is exactly the same for Half Note, Quarter Note and Eighth Note Time Signatures. It is also the same for the rarer Sixteenth Note Time Signatures.

THREE BEATS TO THE BAR

| $\frac{1}{\text{STRONG}}$ 2 WEAK 3 WEAK | $\frac{1}{\text{STRONG}}$ 2 WEAK 3 WEAK | $\frac{1}{\text{STRONG}}$ 2 WEAK 3 WEAK |

$\frac{3}{2} = $ 3 HALF NOTE BEATS TO THE BAR $\frac{3}{4} = $ 3 QUARTER NOTE BEATS TO THE BAR $\frac{3}{8} = $ 3 EIGHTH NOTE BEATS TO THE BAR

FOUR BEATS TO THE BAR

With four Beats to the bar, the first is strong, the second weak, the third medium strong, the fourth weak:

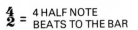

| 1 STRONG 2 MEDIUM WEAK 3 4 WEAK | 1 STRONG 2 MEDIUM WEAK 3 4 WEAK | 1 STRONG 2 MEDIUM WEAK 3 4 WEAK |

$\frac{4}{2} = $ 4 HALF NOTE BEATS TO THE BAR $\mathbf{C}$ OR $\frac{4}{4} = $ 4 QUARTER NOTE BEATS TO THE BAR $\frac{4}{8} = $ 4 EIGHTH NOTE BEATS TO THE BAR

These Time Signatures are for what is known as SIMPLE TIME. We have now covered all the usual Simple Time Signatures and the ways they are counted.

There is another set of Time Signatures for what is known as COMPOUND TIME. Once you know how to count them, they are as easy as the others.

$\frac{6}{8}$ is the one which you are most likely to find. As you would expect, it has six Eighth Notes to the bar.

Count each bar:
   One-two-three-*Two*-two-three, Strong-weak-weak-Medium-weak-weak.
Tap your foot to the underlined beats.

1 STRONG 2 WEAK 3 WEAK 2 MEDIUM 2 WEAK 3 WEAK 1 2 3 2 2 3

Often, $^6_8$ music is fairly fast. Then, we only count Eighth Notes where they are written.

1   2   1 2 3   2 2 3   1 2 3   2

$^6_4$ — six Quarter Notes — and $^6_{16}$ — six Sixteenth Notes — work in the same way. Count all six notes if the music is slow, or if you need to work out the timing, otherwise just count two main beats.

If you tap your foot in time with the beat, only tap the underlined beats with Compound Time Signatures.

Try to understand how all the Time Signatures work because they will help you to play or sing with the correct rhythm and feeling. When you come across one which you don't remember, or if you are not sure about the rhythm, come back and look it up in these pages. Use the examples shown here to help you work out the timing of the notes.

$^9_8$ has nine Eighth Note notes to the bar, which go:

Strong-weak-weak-Medium-weak-weak-Medium-weak-weak.

If you need to work out the timing of Eighth Notes count all nine notes, otherwise only count the three main beats:

1   2   3   1 2 3   2 2 3   3 2 3

62

You will not often come across $\frac{9}{4}$ — nine Quarter Notes — or $\frac{9}{16}$ — nine Sixteenth Notes — but they can be counted in the same way:

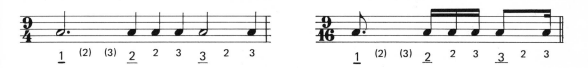

$\frac{12}{8}$ has twelve Eighth Notes notes in each bar. Count only the four beats unless you need to work out the timing of notes.

$\frac{12}{4}$ — a very rare Time Signature — and $\frac{12}{16}$ are counted in the same way.

Occasionally, Time Signatures such as $\frac{5}{4}$ or $\frac{7}{8}$ may be found. $\frac{5}{4}$ has five Quarter Note beats to the bar and $\frac{7}{8}$ has seven Eighth Note beats to the bar. Any others can be worked out in the same way.

The Time Signature may change in the middle of a piece of music. The new Time is written on the Stave where the change is to take place. From that point, there will be a different number of beats to the bar and a new rhythm.

Two Time Signatures at the beginning of music warn us that some bars will have one number of beats and other bars a different number of beats.

Finally, the rhythm of music may be changed for just one bar, or for the whole piece, by various signs including: Rests, Dotted Notes, Tied Notes, Slurs, Triplets, Pauses or Accents. (Accents are explained in later pages.)

GREENSLEEVES, an old English love song, is written here in $\frac{6}{8}$ Time. As you can see, it has some Dotted Eighth Notes and Sixteenth Notes. The timing is given to help you to read it. Chord Symbols are also shown.

64

Minor Keys

There is another set of Keys which are known as the MINOR KEYS. Music in these Keys usually has a rather sad or mournful feeling — in contrast to the happier, brighter mood of Major Keys.

Music in a Minor Key is based on the notes of a Minor Scale. Here is a Scale for the Key of A Minor. If you can, play it on any instrument and hear the sombre effect of a Minor Scale:

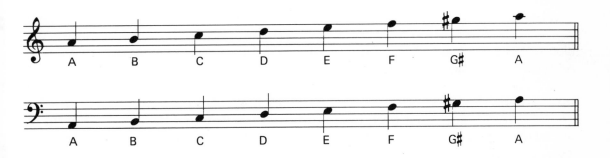

Minor Keys have the same Key Signature as the Major Key which is most similar.

The Key Signature with no Sharps or Flats is shared by C Major and A Minor. (This is in spite of the G♯ found in the Scale of A Minor. The seventh note of the Minor Scale is usually, but not always, sharpened in Music in a Minor Key. It does not appear in the Key Signature, but is written in as an 'Accidental' when needed.)

The two Keys with the same Key Signature are said to be RELATIVE to each other—

A Minor is the RELATIVE MINOR to C Major.

C is the RELATIVE MAJOR to A Minor.

When written, the word 'Minor' is often shortened to a small 'm' — 'Am' means A Minor.

The Key Signatures and Scales of all the Major Keys and their Relative Minor Keys are shown on pages 70-74.

65

It may seem a little confusing to have two Keys with the same Key Signature, but it does not necessarily have to concern you. If you like, you can read all music by following the Sharps or Flats in the Key Signature and changing notes marked by 'Accidental' signs — without worrying about which Key it is in. However, you will understand music better, and play or sing it better, if you know whether it is in a Major or Minor Key.

Major and Minor Keys are not the same, in spite of having the same Key Signatures. Notes run in different patterns in Minor Keys, giving a different effect and feeling. The melody is written around and leads back to a different Key Note, and the extra 'Accidental' note may be used. Music in a Minor Key has different chords accompanying it — mainly Minor Chords. So, how do we find out whether music is in a Major or Minor Key?

Some music is named after the Key in which it is written. 'Prelude in G' means that the Prelude, or most of it, was written in the Key of G Major. 'Concerto in Cm' was written in C Minor, and so on. Musicians also refer to Keys when they say 'I play that tune in E♭' — meaning the Key of E Flat Major.

Sometimes the Key is marked on the music. If it isn't, you can usually work it out by looking at the last chord, or last note. (If there is an accompaniment on the Bass Stave, the lowest note there is a good guide.) For example, with no Sharps or Flats in the Key Signature, the music can only be in C Major or A Minor. If the last note is A, or the last chord is A Minor, then the music is likely to be in A Minor, not C Major.

Look back to 'Greensleeves' on page 64. The Key Signature has no Sharps or Flats, but it is in the Key of A Minor, rather than C Major — because the last note is A and the last chord is A Minor.

You can work out the Keys for most music in this way. It isn't difficult — each Key Signature can only be for one of two Keys, one Major and one Minor. You can look up the Key Signatures for all Keys on pages 70-74 to help you. After a while, you will know which patterns of notes and chords to expect in each Key. Then you will be well on the way to being able to read almost any piece of music straight away.

The next tune is a Christmas carol called 'God Rest You Merry, Gentlemen'. It is written here in the Key of D Minor which has one Flat — the same Key Signature as F Major.

GOD REST YOU MERRY, GENTLEMEN
Every B should be flattened with this Key Signature.

E♯, B♯ and Double Sharps (✗)

In some rare Sharp Keys, you may come across the notes E Sharp and B Sharp, and even notes which are called 'Double Sharps'. However, they are not new notes, only different names for notes which you already know.

E Sharp is another name for F Natural.

Certain Keys need the note F Sharp *and* the note we normally call 'F Natural'. In these Keys, 'F Natural' is renamed 'E Sharp' to keep the names of notes in the Scales in alphabetical order, and allow Key Signatures to be written. (The same note cannot be both Sharp and Natural in a Key Signature.)

B Sharp is the name sometimes given to C Natural for similar reasons.

A DOUBLE SHARP SIGN (✗) further sharpens a note which is already Sharp. The note marked is usually one of the Sharps in the Key Signature. The sign (✗) raises the note to what would normally be the Natural note above.

Here, 'F Double Sharp' is the note normally called 'G Natural'.

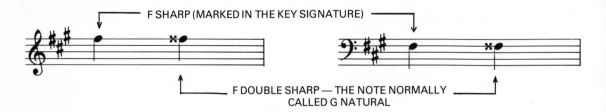

A Double Sharp is cancelled (or to use the correct musical term 'contradicted') by a Natural Sharp sign (♮♯) in front of the note. The note then returns to being a normal Sharp note.

Double Sharps are written in when needed as 'Accidentals'. They affect the note marked for the rest of the bar, unless contradicted (cancelled) by the sign ♮♯.

The alternative names of all notes are shown at the bottom of the opposite page.

C♭, F♭ and Double Flats (♭♭)

In a few rare Flat Keys, you may find the notes C Flat and F Flat and notes called 'Double Flats'. These are different names for notes which you already know:
C Flat is another name for B Natural.
F Flat is another name for E Natural.
In certain Keys, these notes are renamed to keep the names of notes in the Scales in alphabetical order and allow Key Signatures to be written.

A DOUBLE FLAT SIGN (♭♭) further flattens a note which is already flat. The note marked is usually one of the Flats in the Key Signature. The sign (♭♭) lowers the note to what would normally be the Natural note below.

Here, 'B Double Flat' is the note normally called 'A Natural'.

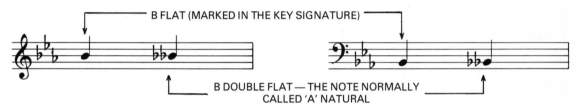

A Double Flat is contradicted (cancelled) by a Natural Flat sign (♮♭) in front of the note. The note then returns to being a normal Flat note.

Double Flats are written in when needed as 'Accidentals'. They affect the note marked for the rest of the bar, unless contradicted by the sign ♮♭.

ALTERNATIVE NAMES FOR NOTES
The different names which notes may have are shown here on the Keyboard, but the notes have the same alternative names on other instruments. Refer to them here when necessary.

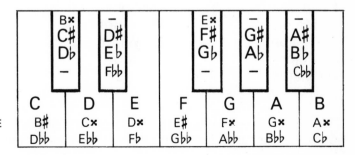

	C	D	E	F	G	A	B
DOUBLE SHARP (✖) NAME	B✖	—		E✖	—	—	
SHARP (♯) NAME	C♯	D♯		F♯	G♯	A♯	
FLAT (♭) NAME	D♭	E♭		G♭	A♭	B♭	
DOUBLE FLAT (♭♭) NAME	—	F♭♭		—	—	C♭♭	
NATURAL NAME	C	D	E	F	G	A	B
SHARP (♯) OR DOUBLE SHARP (✖) NAME	B♯	C✖	D✖	E♯	F✖	G✖	A✖
FLAT (♭) OR DOUBLE FLAT (♭♭) NAME	D♭♭	E♭♭	F♭	G♭♭	A♭♭	B♭♭	C♭

All the Keys — Major and Minor

Key Signatures for all the Major and Minor Keys are shown here, including some which are very rarely used. It isn't necessary to learn them all — you can look them up here when you come across any which you don't know.

Remember that the Sharp or Flat Signs in Key Signatures affect every note with the same name as the ones marked. The signs apply from the beginning to the end of the music, except where extra 'Accidental' Sharp, Flat or Natural signs are written in, or there is a change of Key.

The Sharp and Flat Signs of Key Signatures are always shown in the same order in the same positions on the Staves. The names of these Sharps and Flats are given here above each Key Signature in the order they appear on the Staves.

Major and Minor Scales are shown for each Key for those who find them helpful. The Minor Scales are actually the 'Harmonic Minor Scales' upon which most music in Minor Keys is based. The seventh notes of these Scales are 'Accidental' Sharp or Natural notes which are not in the Key Signatures. These 'Accidentals' are to be found in some, but not all music in Minor Keys.

If you have any doubts about Key Signatures or Scales, refer to 'Keys and Key Signatures' on pages 34-38 or 'Minor Keys' on page 65.

MAJOR KEY	RELATIVE MINOR KEY	KEY SIGNATURE
A Major	F♯ Minor	3 Sharps
B♭ Major	G Minor	2 Flats
B Major	G♯ Minor	5 Sharps
*C♭ Major	A♭ Minor	7 Flats
C Major	A Minor	No Sharps or Flats
C♯ Major	A♯ Minor	7 Sharps
D♭ Major	B♭ Minor	5 Flats
D Major	B Minor	2 Sharps
E♭ Major	C Minor	3 Flats
E Major	C♯ Minor	4 Sharps
F Major	D Minor	One Flat
F♯ Major	D♯ Minor	6 Sharps
G♭ Major	E♭ Minor	6 Flats
G Major	E Minor	One Sharp
A♭ Major	F Minor	4 Flats

*C♭ Major is not used. Nor are the Keys of A♯ Major, D♯ Major, G♯ Major, D♭ Minor or G♭ Minor.

NO SHARPS OR FLATS — The Keys of C Major and A Minor.

Scale of C MAJOR: C D E F G A B C
Scale of A MINOR: A B C D E F G♯ A

SHARP KEYS

ONE SHARP — The Keys of G Major and E Minor.
F♯ is in the Key Signature.

Scale of G MAJOR: G A B C D E F♯ G
Scale of E MINOR: E F♯ G A B C D♯ E

TWO SHARPS — The Keys of D Major and B Minor.
F♯ and C♯ are in the Key Signature.

Scale of D MAJOR: D E F♯ G A B C♯ D
Scale of B MINOR: B C♯ D E F♯ G A♯ B

THREE SHARPS — The Keys of A Major and F♯ Minor.
F♯, C♯ and G♯ are in the Key Signature.

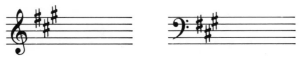

Scale of A MAJOR: A B C♯ D E F♯ G♯ A
Scale of F♯ MINOR: F♯ G♯ A B C♯ D E♯ F♯
                                    *

* The note E Sharp is explained on page 68.

FOUR SHARPS — The Keys of E Major and C♯ Minor.
F♯, C♯, G♯ and D♯ are in the Key Signature.

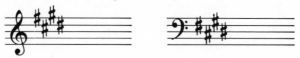

Scale of E MAJOR: E F♯ G♯ A B C♯ D♯ E
Scale of C♯ MINOR: C♯ D♯ E F♯ G♯ A B♯ C♯
*

FIVE SHARPS — The Keys of B Major and G♯ Minor.
F♯, C♯, G♯, D♯ and A♯ are in the Key Signature.

Scale of B MAJOR: B C♯ D♯ E F♯ G♯ A♯ B
Scale of G♯ MINOR: G♯ A♯ B C♯ D♯ E F✗ G♯
*

SIX SHARPS — The Keys of F♯ Major and D♯ Minor.
These Keys are very rarely used.
F♯, C♯, G♯, D♯, A♯ and E♯ are in the Key Signature.

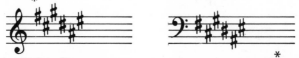

Scale of F♯ MAJOR: F♯ G♯ A♯ B C♯ D♯ E♯ F♯
Scale of D♯ MINOR: D♯ E♯ F♯ G♯ A♯ B C✗ D♯
*   *

SEVEN SHARPS — The Keys of C♯ Major and A♯ Minor.
These Keys are very rarely used.
All the Sharps are in the Key Signature — F♯, C♯, G♯, D♯, A♯, E♯ and B♯.

Scale of C♯ MAJOR: C♯ D♯ E♯ F♯ G♯ A♯ B♯ C♯
Scale of A♯ MINOR: A♯ B♯ C♯ D♯ E♯ F♯ G✗ A♯
*   *   *

*The notes E Sharp, B Sharp and Double Sharps (✗) are explained on page 68.

FLAT KEYS

ONE FLAT — The Keys of F Major and D Minor.
B♭ is in the Key Signature.

Scale of F MAJOR: F G A B♭ C D E F
Scale of D MINOR: D E F G A B♭ C♯ D

TWO FLATS — The Keys of B♭ Major and G Minor.
B♭ and E♭ are in the Key Signature.

Scale of B♭ MAJOR: B♭ C D E♭ F G A B♭
Scale of G MINOR: G A B♭ C D E♭ F♯ G

THREE FLATS — The Keys of E♭ Major and C Minor.
B♭, E♭ and A♭ are in the Key Signature.

Scale of E♭ MAJOR: E♭ F G A♭ B♭ C D E♭
Scale of C MINOR: C D E♭ F G A♭ B♮ C
                                            *

FOUR FLATS — The Keys of A♭ Major and F Minor.
B♭, E♭, A♭ and D♭ are in the Key Signature.

Scale of A♭ MAJOR: A♭ B♭ C D♭ E♭ F G A♭
Scale of F MINOR: F G A♭ B♭ C D♭ E♮ F
                                          *

*The Natural sign (♮) in these Minor Scales contradicts (cancels) the Flat in the Key Signature.

FIVE FLATS — The Keys of D♭ Major and B♭ Minor.
B♭, E♭, A♭, D♭ and G♭ are in the Key Signature.

Scale of D♭ MAJOR: D♭ E♭ F G♭ A♭ B♭ C D♭
Scale of B♭ MINOR: B♭ C D♭ E♭ F G♭ A♮ B♭
　　　　　　　　　　　　　　　　　　　*

SIX FLATS — The Keys of G♭ Major and E♭ Minor.
B♭, E♭, A♭, D♭, G♭ and C♭ are in the Key Signature.

Scale of G♭ MAJOR: G♭ A♭ B♭ C♭ D♭ E♭ F G♭
Scale of E♭ MINOR: E♭ F G♭ A♭ B♭ C♭ D♮ E♭
　　　　　　　　　　　　　　　　　　⊛　*

SEVEN FLATS — The Keys of C♭ Major and A♭ Minor.
The Key of C♭ Major is not used because notes which sound the same are in the simpler Key of B Major.
All the Flats are in the Key Signatures — B♭, E♭, A♭, D♭, G♭, C♭ and F♭

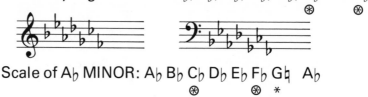

Scale of A♭ MINOR: A♭ B♭ C♭ D♭ E♭ F♭ G♮ A♭
　　　　　　　　　　　　⊛　　　⊛　*

*The Natural sign (♮) in these Minor Scales contradicts (cancels) the Flat in the Key Signature.

⊛The notes C Flat and F Flat are explained on page 69.

Key Signatures for the C Clef (𝄡) are shown on page 84.

Octaves and Octave Signs (8ve)

OCTAVE, which comes from the Greek word for 'eight', is a term often used by musicians and singers. An Octave is the distance between two notes with the same name, eight notes apart in a Scale.

From one C to the next C higher is an Octave:

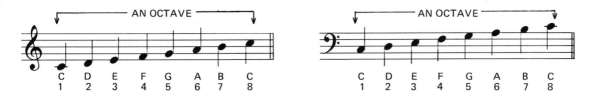

The second C is an OCTAVE HIGHER than the first C — because it is eight notes higher up the Scale.

The first C is an OCTAVE LOWER than the second C.

Continuing, we come to the note with the same name TWO OCTAVES HIGHER.

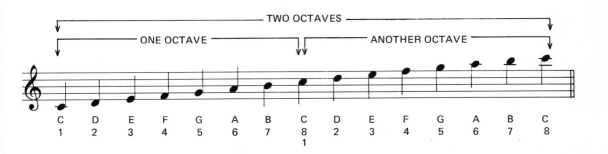

The same applies to all notes —
From one D to the next D higher is an Octave;
From E to the next E higher is an Octave, and so on.

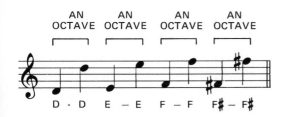

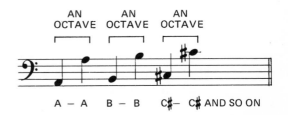

75

A few notes or a few bars of music are sometimes shown an Octave higher or lower than they are played or sung, to make them easier to read. The notes which are to be higher or lower are marked with an Octave sign —

8ve .... or 8va .... or 8 ....

An Octave sign *over* notes means they should be played or sung an Octave *higher*.

WRITTEN   PLAYED OR SUNG

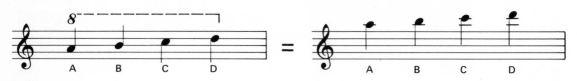

An Octave sign *under* notes means they should be played an Octave *lower*.

WRITTEN   PLAYED

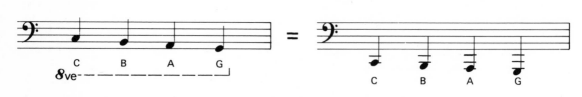

'Con 8' or 'Con 8ve' under a note, tells us that the written note *and* the note an Octave lower are to be played together. ('Con' means 'with'.)

WRITTEN   PLAYED

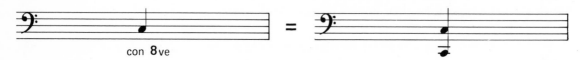

Octaves also describe the range of notes which can be played or sung by an instrument or voice — the Piano usually has a range of seven Octaves, a human voice has a range of about two Octaves. All the notes — Naturals, Sharps and Flats — between two notes an Octave apart are said to be 'in the same Octave'.

76

Other Signs which affect notes

There are some signs which affect the way notes are played or sung. You will not necessarily come across these signs in your music, but look them up here, or in the Directory of Musical Signs at the back of the book, if you do.

 A dot above or below a note means it should be STACCATO — played or sung shortly and sharply — with a silent space between the note and the next note.

 A dash above or below a note means it should be *very* short and sharply played — with a silent space before the next note.

 The curved line (or Slur) with dots tells us that these notes should be less Staccato, but still be separated by silent spaces.

 A Strong Accent.
The note marked should be played or sung strongly, but not cut short like 'Staccato'.

rf, sf, sfz The note marked is to be given special emphasis.

 The note marked should be played or sung firmly.

 A curved line over two different notes means the second note should be slightly shorter and weaker.

GRACE NOTES (or Ornaments) are extra notes added to music for effect. They are often a decoration which is not essential to the music.

 A small note with a stroke across the tail should be played or sung as quickly as possible *before the beat* of the full size note which follows.

 If the small note has no stroke across the tail, it is played or sung *on the beat*. It has the same value (length) as a full size note of the same shape, and it shortens the note which follows to half its normal length. This example sounds the same as two eighth notes.

 Sometimes, several small notes are written together. They have the same value as full size notes, and shorten the main note which follows to half its normal length.

tr. OR
tr ～～～ A TRILL (or SHAKE). The written note and the note above are played many times, one after the other, very quickly. The exact number of times it is played depends on the player. The Trill lasts for the same number of beats as the written note — and ends on the written note.

WRITTEN　　　　　　　　　PLAYED APPROXIMATELY LIKE THIS

The Trill sign is also used to indicate a 'roll' on the drums.

∽ OR ～ The TURN. Four notes are played or sung in this order: (1) the note *above* the written note, (2) the written note, (3) the note below, (4) the written note again.

Written over a note, it is played or sung like this:

WRITTEN　　　　　　　　　PLAYED OR SUNG

Between two notes, it acts as a link, shortening the note before it:

WRITTEN　　　　　　　　　PLAYED OR SUNG

∾ OR **S**
↲ OR ～ An INVERTED TURN starts on the note *below* instead. It is played or sung in this order: (1) The note below the written note, (2) the written note, (3) the note above, (4) the written note again.

WRITTEN　　　　　　　　　PLAYED

The MORDENT. Two extra, softer notes are played or sung very quickly before the written note. The extra notes are the written note and the note above.

The LOWER MORDENT. The Mordent sign with a stroke (𝄿) tells us that the written note and the note *below* are needed.

WRITTEN   PLAYED OR SUNG

MORDENT   LOWER   MORDENT   LOWER MORDENT
           MORDENT

If any of these Grace Notes or Ornaments are to use Sharp, Flat or Natural notes which are not in the Key Signature, a ♯, ♭ or ♮ sign is written above the Grace Note sign, or in front of the Grace Note. A ♯,♭ or ♮ sign *over* a Turn sign (𝄾) affects the note *above* the written note, below the sign (𝄾) it affects the note below.

Other numbers of notes may be grouped together in the same way as the Triplet described on page 58. However, you are not likely to find these very often.

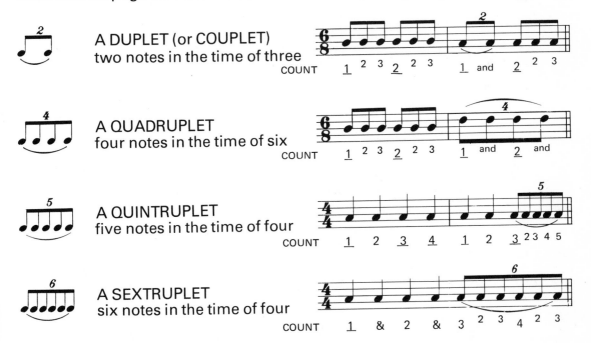

A DUPLET (or COUPLET)
two notes in the time of three

COUNT   1 2 3 2 2 3   1 and 2 2 3

A QUADRUPLET
four notes in the time of six

COUNT   1 2 3 2 2 3   1 and 2 and

A QUINTRUPLET
five notes in the time of four

COUNT   1 2 3 4   1 2 3 2 3 4 5

A SEXTRUPLET
six notes in the time of four

COUNT   1 & 2 & 3 2 3 4 2 3

The timing of any other numbers of notes can be worked out in similar ways.

Notes which are to be repeated

The 'Musical Shorthand' or Abbreviations described earlier in the book are sometimes used if a large part of a piece of music is to be repeated. Other less usual Abbreviations save reading the same notes or rests several times. These Abbreviations use strokes (*I*) in different ways to tell us that notes, rests or even whole bars are to be repeated. If you come across them, look them up here.

Strokes written on the Stave mean that a group of notes is to be played or sung more than once. One stroke is used for each time the notes are repeated:

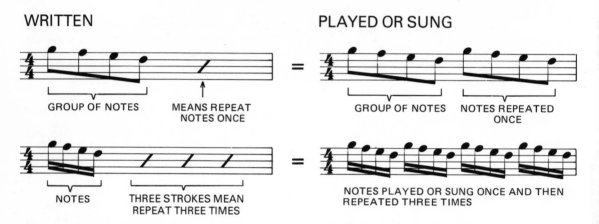

WRITTEN

GROUP OF NOTES — MEANS REPEAT NOTES ONCE

PLAYED OR SUNG

GROUP OF NOTES — NOTES REPEATED ONCE

NOTES — THREE STROKES MEAN REPEAT THREE TIMES

NOTES PLAYED OR SUNG ONCE AND THEN REPEATED THREE TIMES

BARS TO BE REPEATED

Whole bars which are to be repeated are marked with this sign: ✕.

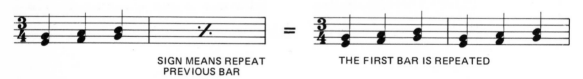

SIGN MEANS REPEAT PREVIOUS BAR

THE FIRST BAR IS REPEATED

Two bars are to be repeated if the sign is written across the Bar-Line:

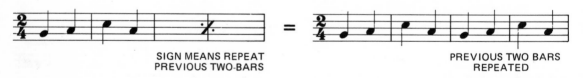

SIGN MEANS REPEAT PREVIOUS TWO-BARS

PREVIOUS TWO BARS REPEATED

REPEATED RESTS

If a rest is to last for a long time — which often happens in Orchestral music — a special sign may give the number of bars it is to last.

= TWELVE BARS REST

SINGLE NOTES AND CHORDS WHICH ARE TO BE REPEATED

A stroke over or under a note or chord tells us it is to be played several times as Eighth Notes. The number of Eighth Notes to be played depends on the length of the note which is written.
If it is a Whole Note with a stroke (𝄽), we would play 8 Eighth Notes;
If it is a Half Note (𝅗𝅥), we would play 4 Eighth Notes;
If it is a Quarter Note (𝅘𝅥), we would play 2 Eighth Notes:

WRITTEN   PLAYED

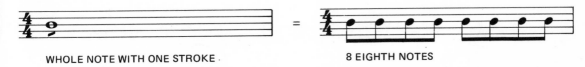

WHOLE NOTE WITH ONE STROKE   8 EIGHTH NOTES

Sometimes, more than one note is to be repeated. Here the first note is played the correct number of times before going on to the next note:

FIRST NOTE   SECOND NOTE   FIRST NOTE   SECOND NOTE

EACH HALF NOTE = 4 EIGHTH NOTES

Two strokes (𝄿) tell us that the notes should be played as Sixteenth Notes:

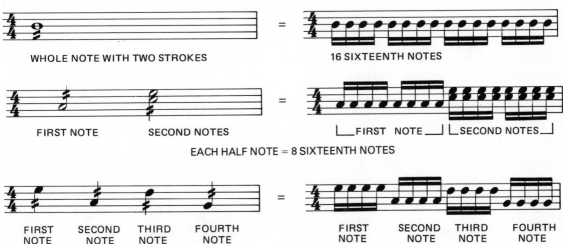

WHOLE NOTE WITH TWO STROKES   16 SIXTEENTH NOTES

FIRST NOTE   SECOND NOTES   FIRST NOTE   SECOND NOTES

EACH HALF NOTE = 8 SIXTEENTH NOTES

FIRST   SECOND   THIRD   FOURTH   FIRST   SECOND   THIRD   FOURTH
NOTE   NOTE   NOTE   NOTE   NOTE   NOTE   NOTE   NOTE

EACH QUARTER NOTE = 4 SIXTEENTH NOTES

With three strokes (𝄿), each note is played as Thirty-Second Notes (each Half Note = 16 Thirty-Second Notes, and so on).
With Four strokes (𝄿), each note is played as Sixty-Fourth Notes.

Eighth notes marked with one stroke mean that 2 Sixteenth Notes are to be played or sung for each note marked:

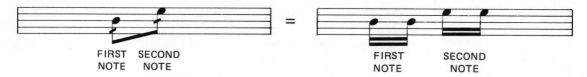

FIRST NOTE   SECOND NOTE   FIRST NOTE   SECOND NOTE

Eighth notes marked with two strokes mean that 4 Thirty-Second Notes are to be played for each of them:

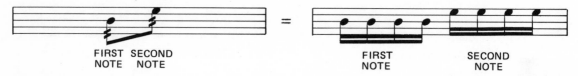

FIRST NOTE   SECOND NOTE   FIRST NOTE   SECOND NOTE

Three strokes means that 8 Sixty-Fourth Notes are to be played for each note marked.

Two Half Notes joined with 'tails' like Eighth Notes are played twice each, one after the other, as Eighth Notes:

WRITTEN   PLAYED

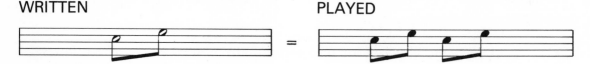

(The total number of Eighth Notes is equal to just one of the Half Notes.)

Two Half Notes with Sixteenth Note 'tails' are played four times each, one after the other, as Sixteenth Notes:

Two Half Notes with Thirty-Second Note 'tails' are played one after the other, eight times each, as Thirty-Second Notes:

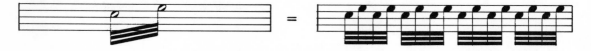

With Sixty-Fourth Note 'tails', they are played sixteen times each.

If 'TREMOLO' or 'trem.' is written above any of these notes, they are to be played as quickly as possible — without worrying about their exact number.

The other Clef — the C Clef (𝄡)

The C Clef is not generally used today except for the viola and occasionally for the cello, bassoon and tenor trombone. The C Clef points to the position of the note called 'Middle C'. Originally, the Clef could be placed on any line of the Stave, each giving a different position for Middle C. These days it is found in two places only:

On the middle line, it is known as the ALTO CLEF, and used for the viola.

MIDDLE C → C

The notes higher and lower than Middle C run in order up and down the Stave.

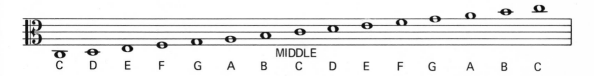

C D E F G A B MIDDLE C D E F G A B C

On the fourth line it is known as the TENOR CLEF, which is sometimes used for the higher notes on the 'cello, bassoon and tenor trombone.

MIDDLE C → C

The notes run up and down the Stave from Middle C on the fourth line.

A B C D E F G A B MIDDLE C D E F G A

All the signs which are to be found in music with the other Clefs may be used with the C Clef in either position.

83

KEY SIGNATURES FOR THE C CLEF

Key Signatures for the Alto and Tenor Clefs are similar to those for the other Clefs — but the Sharp and Flat signs are in different positions.

If you have any doubts about Key Signatures, or want to know the notes in any Scales, refer to pages 34-38, 65-66 or 70-74.

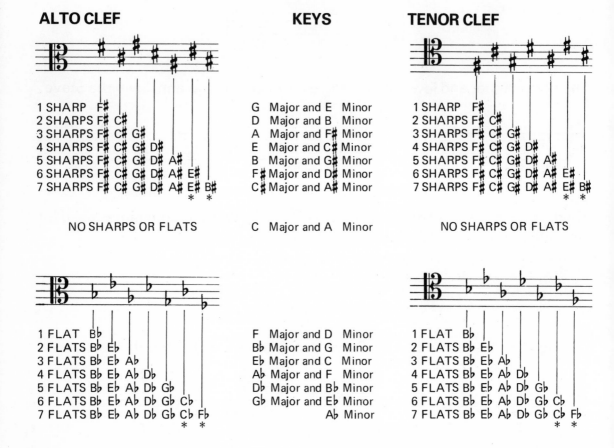

ALTO CLEF

1 SHARP	F♯
2 SHARPS	F♯ C♯
3 SHARPS	F♯ C♯ G♯
4 SHARPS	F♯ C♯ G♯ D♯
5 SHARPS	F♯ C♯ G♯ D♯ A♯
6 SHARPS	F♯ C♯ G♯ D♯ A♯ E♯
7 SHARPS	F♯ C♯ G♯ D♯ A♯ E♯ B♯
	* *

NO SHARPS OR FLATS

1 FLAT	B♭
2 FLATS	B♭ E♭
3 FLATS	B♭ E♭ A♭
4 FLATS	B♭ E♭ A♭ D♭
5 FLATS	B♭ E♭ A♭ D♭ G♭
6 FLATS	B♭ E♭ A♭ D♭ G♭ C♭
7 FLATS	B♭ E♭ A♭ D♭ G♭ C♭ F♭
	* *

KEYS

G	Major and E	Minor
D	Major and B	Minor
A	Major and F♯	Minor
E	Major and C♯	Minor
B	Major and G♯	Minor
F♯	Major and D♯	Minor
C♯	Major and A♯	Minor

C   Major and A   Minor

F	Major and D	Minor
B♭	Major and G	Minor
E♭	Major and C	Minor
A♭	Major and F	Minor
D♭	Major and B♭	Minor
G♭	Major and E♭	Minor
		A♭	Minor

TENOR CLEF

1 SHARP	F♯
2 SHARPS	F♯ C♯
3 SHARPS	F♯ C♯ G♯
4 SHARPS	F♯ C♯ G♯ D♯
5 SHARPS	F♯ C♯ G♯ D♯ A♯
6 SHARPS	F♯ C♯ G♯ D♯ A♯ E♯
7 SHARPS	F♯ C♯ G♯ D♯ A♯ E♯ B♯
	* *

NO SHARPS OR FLATS

1 FLAT	B♭
2 FLATS	B♭ E♭
3 FLATS	B♭ E♭ A♭
4 FLATS	B♭ E♭ A♭ D♭
5 FLATS	B♭ E♭ A♭ D♭ G♭
6 FLATS	B♭ E♭ A♭ D♭ G♭ C♭
7 FLATS	B♭ E♭ A♭ D♭ G♭ C♭ F♭
	* *

*The notes E♯, B♯, C♭ and F♭ are explained on pages 68-69.

84

Directory of Musical Signs

Look up any signs which you don't remember whenever you come across them — and soon you will find you know the ones you need for your music.

You can get an idea of the meaning of some signs from their shapes and the ways they are used. Curved lines always mean that notes are to be grouped together in some way, Strokes indicate notes or chords which are to be repeated, and so on. Look for the meanings and the signs will be easier to understand.

This Directory may also be used as an index for signs described in this book.

SIGNS ON THE STAVES continued

KEY SIGNATURES — ♯ or ♭ signs placed immediately after the Clef in the positions of notes.

Unless contradicted (cancelled) by Natural signs (♮), they affect every note with the same name as the ones marked.

34-38
70-74
32

TIME SIGNATURES — two numbers, **C** or **₵** which give the number of beats to a Bar.   **C** = 4/4 ,   **₵** = 2/2

24-25
60-63

BAR-LINES. Bar-Lines divide music into Bars. Each Bar has the number of beats indicated by the Time Signature. The first beat after the Bar-Line is usually the strongest beat in the Bar.

15

DOUBLE BAR-LINE. This marks the end of a piece of music, or a Repeat.

15
44

This Double Bar-Line marks the end of a section of music,
— or a change of Key —
— or a change of Time Signature.
It may also mark a Repeat, or the end of the music.

15
37
63
44 & 15

REPEAT SIGNS   see page   44

Repeat the previous Bar. (Sign in middle of Bar)   80

Repeat the previous two Bars. (Sign across Bar-Line)   80

Repeat a chord, or a group of notes. Repeat once for each Stroke.   52 & 80

NOTE SHAPES

SHAPE   VALUE   NAME

𝆏𝅄	2	BREVE. Twice a Whole Note (or Semibreve) 𝆏𝅄 = 𝅝 + 𝅝	57
𝅝	1	WHOLE NOTE (or SEMIBREVE)	
𝅗𝅥 or 𝅗𝅥	½	HALF NOTE (or MINIM) 𝅗𝅥 + 𝅗𝅥 = 𝅝	14-15
𝅘𝅥 or 𝅘𝅥	¼	QUARTER NOTE (or CROTCHET) 𝅘𝅥 + 𝅘𝅥 = 𝅗𝅥	
𝅘𝅥𝅮 or 𝅘𝅥𝅮	⅛	EIGHTH NOTE (or QUAVER) 𝅘𝅥𝅮 + 𝅘𝅥𝅮 = 𝅘𝅥	
𝅘𝅥𝅯 or 𝅘𝅥𝅯	1/16	SIXTEENTH NOTE (or SEMIQUAVER) 𝅘𝅥𝅯 + 𝅘𝅥𝅯 = 𝅘𝅥𝅮	
𝅘𝅥𝅰 or 𝅘𝅥𝅰	1/32	THIRTY-SECOND NOTE (or DEMI-SEMIQUAVER) 𝅘𝅥𝅰 + 𝅘𝅥𝅰 = 𝅘𝅥𝅯	56-57
𝅘𝅥𝅱 or 𝅘𝅥𝅱	1/64	SIXTY-FOURTH NOTE (or SEMI-DEMI-SEMIQUAVER) 𝅘𝅥𝅱 + 𝅘𝅥𝅱 = 𝅘𝅥𝅰	

Here are the notes normally used in relation to one another — and the way they may be counted in a Bar of $\frac{4}{4}$ Time:

1 WHOLE NOTE	𝅝																
	1		2			3			4								
½ HALF NOTE	𝅗𝅥					𝅗𝅥											
	1		2			3			4								
¼ QUARTER NOTE	𝅘𝅥		𝅘𝅥			𝅘𝅥			𝅘𝅥								
	1		2			3			4								
⅛ EIGHTH NOTE	𝅘𝅥𝅮	𝅘𝅥𝅮	𝅘𝅥𝅮 𝅘𝅥𝅮		𝅘𝅥𝅮 𝅘𝅥𝅮		𝅘𝅥𝅮 𝅘𝅥𝅮										
	1	&	2	&	3	&	4	&								
1/16 SIXTEENTH NOTE	𝅘𝅥𝅯 𝅘𝅥𝅯 𝅘𝅥𝅯 𝅘𝅥𝅯		𝅘𝅥𝅯𝅘𝅥𝅯𝅘𝅥𝅯𝅘𝅥𝅯		𝅘𝅥𝅯𝅘𝅥𝅯𝅘𝅥𝅯𝅘𝅥𝅯		𝅘𝅥𝅯𝅘𝅥𝅯𝅘𝅥𝅯𝅘𝅥𝅯										
	1 2 3 4		2 2 3 4		3 2 3 4		4 2 3 4										
1/32 THIRTY-SECOND NOTE	𝅘𝅥𝅰𝅘𝅥𝅰𝅘𝅥𝅰𝅘𝅥𝅰𝅘𝅥𝅰𝅘𝅥𝅰𝅘𝅥𝅰𝅘𝅥𝅰		𝅘𝅥𝅰𝅘𝅥𝅰𝅘𝅥𝅰𝅘𝅥𝅰𝅘𝅥𝅰𝅘𝅥𝅰𝅘𝅥𝅰𝅘𝅥𝅰		𝅘𝅥𝅰𝅘𝅥𝅰𝅘𝅥𝅰𝅘𝅥𝅰𝅘𝅥𝅰𝅘𝅥𝅰𝅘𝅥𝅰𝅘𝅥𝅰		𝅘𝅥𝅰𝅘𝅥𝅰𝅘𝅥𝅰𝅘𝅥𝅰𝅘𝅥𝅰𝅘𝅥𝅰𝅘𝅥𝅰𝅘𝅥𝅰										
	1 & 2 & 3 & 4 &		2 & 2 & 3 & 4 &		3 & 2 & 3 & 4 &		4 & 2 & 3 & 4 &										

NOTE SHAPES continued

These and similar signs are for notes which are to be repeated several times. see pages 81-82

RESTS

Rests last for the same number of beats as the notes which they replace. 20

REST   NOTE

= 𝗼 BREVE REST. 57

= o WHOLE NOTE (or SEMIBREVE) REST. This Rest hangs from the line. It may also indicate a whole bar's rest.

= ♩ HALF NOTE (or MINIM) REST. This Rest sits on the line. } 20

𝄽 or ♩ = ♩ QUARTER NOTE (or CROTCHET) REST. The old-fashioned sign — ♩ — is not often found.

𝄾 = ♪ EIGHTH NOTE (or QUAVER) REST. }

𝄿 = ♬ SIXTEENTH NOTE (or SEMIQUAVER) REST

𝅀 = ♬ THIRTY-SECOND NOTE (or DEMI-SEMIQUAVER) REST. } 57

𝅁 = ♬ SIXTY-FOURTH NOTE (or SEMI-DEMI-SEMIQUAVER) REST.

|— 24 —| Sign used where a rest is to last for a long time. The figure gives the number of bars the rest is to last. 80

DOTS BEHIND NOTES AND RESTS

♩. ♩. ♪. A small dot after a note or rest makes it last half as long again. ♩. = ♩+♩ ♩. = ♩+♪ ♪. = ♪+♬ 22

see examples on pages 25, 62, 56-57

♩.. ♩... Each extra dot adds half as much as the previous dot:

♩.. = ♩+♪+♬   ♩... = ♩+♪+♬+♬ 22

SIGNS IN FRONT OF NOTES

♯ SHARP SIGN. It raises or 'sharpens' a note. It affects all notes in the same position which follow in the bar. Written immediately after the Clef, it is part of the Key Signature.

28-32
34-38
70-74

♭ FLAT SIGN. It lowers or 'flattens' a note. It affects all notes in the same position which follow in the bar. Written immediately after the Clef, it is part of the Key Signature.

28-32
34-38
70-74

♮ NATURAL SIGN. This contradicts (cancels) a ♯ or ♭ — the note marked becomes a 'Natural' note. It affects all notes in the same position which follow in the bar.

32

✖ DOUBLE SHARP SIGN. This further sharpens a note which is already Sharp.   see page

68

♮♯ NATURAL SHARP SIGN. This contradicts (cancels) a Double Sharp sign (✖).   see page

68

♭♭ DOUBLE FLAT SIGN. This further flattens a note which is already Flat.   see page

69

♮♭ NATURAL FLAT SIGN. This contradicts (cancels) a Double Flat sign (♭♭).   see page

69

ARPEGGIO. The notes of the chord are sounded quickly one after the other, starting with the lowest note.

52

GRACE NOTE. Play or sing small note with stroke across it quickly, before the beat of the full size note.

77

GRACE NOTES, without strokes. Play or sing these as if they were full size notes. They shorten the full size note which follows to half its normal length.

77

89

SIGNS OVER OR UNDER NOTES

TIE or BIND, a curved line which lengthens a note by joining it to the next note — if both have the same name and position on the Stave. 21

SLUR, joining several different notes, means they are to be played or sung smoothly. Slurs also indicate 'bowing' for stringed instruments, and 'phrasing'. 21

Two different notes joined by a Slur. The second note is to be slightly shorter and weaker than the first. 77

TRIPLET. Three notes to be fitted into the time of two. Other numbers of notes may be grouped in the same way. 58 79

PAUSE or HOLD SIGN. The note or rest marked is to last longer than normal. May also mark the end of music. 42 45

STACCATO. The note marked is to be short and sharp with a silent space before the next note. 77

Slur (curved line) with dots means the notes are less Staccato, but still separated by silent spaces. 77

DASH. The note marked is to be very short and sharp. 77

A Strong Accent. Play or sing the note strongly. 77

Play or sing the note firmly. 77

rf   *sf*   *sfz*   The note is to be given special emphasis. 77

8^{ve} 8va 8   OCTAVE SIGN. Shown over notes, play or sing an Octave higher. Under notes, play or sing an Octave lower. 75-76

con 8^{ve} con 8   Play written note *and* note an Octave lower, together. 75-76

Ped. ⌐   PEDAL. Press down the right pedal on the piano. 105

V   ⊓   BOWING AND PLUCKING SIGNS for stringed instruments. V = up, ⊓ = down.

90

trem.	TREMOLO	82
tr or tr ⌇⌇⌇	TRILL or SHAKE	
⌇⌇ ⌇⌇	MORDENTS	Signs for Musical Ornaments
∽ ～⌇	TURNS	see pages 78-79

SIGNS ABOVE OR BELOW THE STAVES

♩ = 76, etc.	Tempo sign giving the exact number of beats to a minute.	42
D.C.	DA CAPO. Repeat from the beginning.	
D.S., 𝄋	DAL SEGNO. Repeat from the sign — 𝄋	
⊕	CODA SIGN. 'Al Coda' means go to the Coda (marked ⊕).	44-45
D.S. al Coda	Repeat from sign 𝄋 until ⊕ , then go to Coda.	
⌐1 ⌐2	FIRST and SECOND TIME BARS.	
rall., ritard.	RALLENTANDO, RITARDANDO. Slow down gradually.	42
rit.,	RITENUTO. Held back — slightly slower.	42
Accel.	ACCELERANDO. Speed up gradually.	42

◁ or cresc.	CRESCENDO. Gradually become louder.	
▷ or dim..	DIMINUENDO. Gradually become softer.	
p	PIANO, softly	
pp	PIANISSIMO, very softly	
ppp	PIANISSISSIMO, as quietly as possible.	
mp	MEZZO-PIANO, moderately softly.	
m	MEZZO, medium. 'Mezzo' means 'half'.	43
mf	MEZZO-FORTE, moderately loudly.	
f	FORTE, loudly.	
ff	FORTISSIMO, very loudly.	
fff	FORTISSISSIMO, as loudly as possible.	
pf	PIU FORTE, more loudly.	
fp	FORTEPIANO, a quick change from loud to soft.	

Other words may be looked up in the Dictionary on pages 95 to 112.

Note Directory

Use this page and the next to look up notes on the Treble and Bass Staves for all voices and instruments, except the guitar. Notes for the guitar are shown on page 94.

See pages 68 and 69 for the notes E♯, B♯, C♭, F♭ and Double Sharps (𝄪) and Double Flats (♭♭).

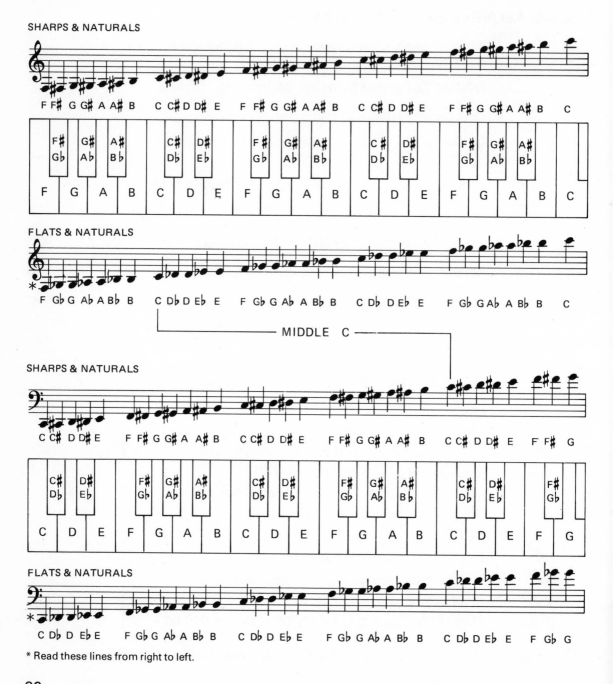

SHARPS & NATURALS

FLATS & NATURALS

MIDDLE C

SHARPS & NATURALS

FLATS & NATURALS

* Read these lines from right to left.

NOTES ON LEGER LINES

Any of these notes may be affected by Accidental Sharps, Flats, Naturals, Double Sharps or Double Flats — or by Sharp or Flat signs in Key Signatures.

You are not likely to find more Leger Lines than those shown. If you do, work them out as explained on page 17.

Notes which are two or more Leger Lines below the Treble Stave also appear on the Bass Stave. Notes two or more Leger Lines above the Bass Stave also appear on the Treble Stave (see pages 17 & 19.)

TREBLE STAVE

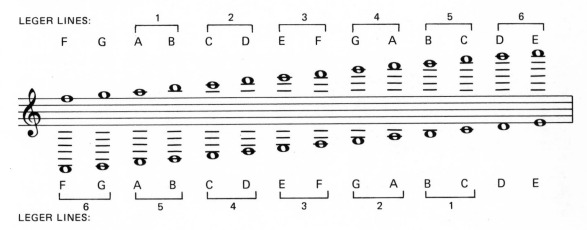

BASS STAVE

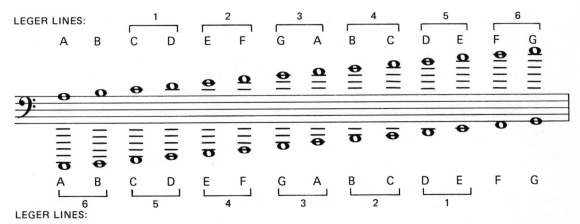

Notes on the Guitar

For the notes E♯, B♯, C♭, F♭ and Double Sharps (✘) and Double Flats (♭♭) see pages 68-69

In guitar music, notes which are to be played above the fourth fret are often marked with small circled numbers — ② ③ ④ and so on. These give the number of the string on which the note is to be played.

Music for the guitar is always written an Octave higher than it sounds —

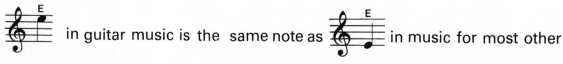

in guitar music is the same note as ... in music for most other instruments. If you read music for other instruments, it is often best to play it exactly as it is written.

A Short Musical Dictionary

This short Dictionary gives the Musical Terms which you are most likely to find when reading music. It also serves as an Index for this book. Use it to look up anything you may have forgotten or don't understand.

Italian words are marked (It.) and Latin words (Lat.). Normal English words which have the same meaning in music are not included. Any other words may be found in a full musical dictionary or, in the case of foreign words, in a dictionary of the language concerned.

Alto. The lowest voices of women and boys. Also instruments which play the notes of these voices.

Alto Clef. The C Clef giving the position of the note Middle C on the middle line of the Stave. ← MIDDLE C

83

Andante (It.). At a moderate pace. Andante means 'walking'.

Andantino (It.). A little faster than Andante.

Animato (It.). Animated, lively, spirited.

A piacere (It.). At pleasure. The speed of the music is left for the player or singer to decide.

A poco a poco (It.). Little by little. Used for a change of Tempo (Speed) or Volume.

A poco più lento (It.). A little slower.

A poco più mosso (It.). A little more movement — a little faster.

Appassionata (It.). With passion.

Arrangement. Music which has been changed from the original way in which it was written. It may be in a different Key, simpler or more complex, or it may be adapted to suit different voices or instruments. Music which is arranged for an instrument or voice is particularly suitable for that instrument or voice.

Arco (It.). Bow. 'Arco' written above or below the Stave indicates that stringed instruments, such as the violin, are to use bows instead of plucking the strings (pizzicato).

Aria (It.). An air or tune.

Arpeggio (It.). The notes of a chord sounded very quickly, one after the other, starting with the lowest note. Arpeggios are marked by signs ≬ or (in front of chords.

52

A Tempo (It.). Play or sing in time. Go back to original speed.

Bar or Measure. The space between two Bar-Lines. Each bar contains the number of beats shown by the Time Signature.

A BAR
OR MEASURE

15

Baritone. Voices and instruments halfway between Tenor and Bass.

Bar-Line. A vertical line across the Stave. Bar-Lines divide music into bars, each of which has the number of beats shown by the Time Signature.

15

The first beat after the Bar-Line is usually the strongest beat in the bar.

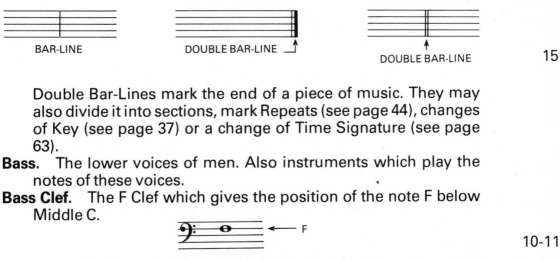

| BAR-LINE | DOUBLE BAR-LINE ⌐↑ | DOUBLE BAR-LINE ↑ |

15

Double Bar-Lines mark the end of a piece of music. They may also divide it into sections, mark Repeats (see page 44), changes of Key (see page 37) or a change of Time Signature (see page 63).

Bass. The lower voices of men. Also instruments which play the notes of these voices.

Bass Clef. The F Clef which gives the position of the note F below Middle C.

10-11

Beat. The rhythm to which you tap your foot in time with music. Also the rhythm of each bar which may be counted.

Some beats are stronger than others.

14
25

Ben (It.). Well. Ben Marcato = well marked, make the melody stand out clearly.

Bind or Tie. A curved line (⌒ or ‿) which lengthens a note by joining it to the next note — if both notes have the same name and position on the Stave. The first note lasts for the combined number of beats of the notes 'tied' together. A curved line which links different notes is not a Tie, but a Slur (see pages 21 and 77).

21

Bis (Lat.). The part marked is to be played or sung twice.

Brace. A bracket and line which joins two or more Staves of music. Music joined together in this way is to be played at the same time by one instrument, or one group of instruments, or a group of voices.

OR

48-49

Breve. Twice a Whole Note (or Semibreve). The Breve is the longest note. It is not often found except in Church music.

The Breve is written ꞏ▯ꞏ , the Breve Rest: ▬ OR ▬

57

Brillante (It.). Bright, brilliant.

Brio   (It.).   Vigour. Con brio = with vigour, strongly, energetically.

Calando   (It.).   Dying away, becoming slower and softer.
Cantabile   (It.). ⎫
Cantando   (It.). ⎭   As if singing.

C Clef.   The Alto or Tenor Clef which gives the position of the note Middle C.

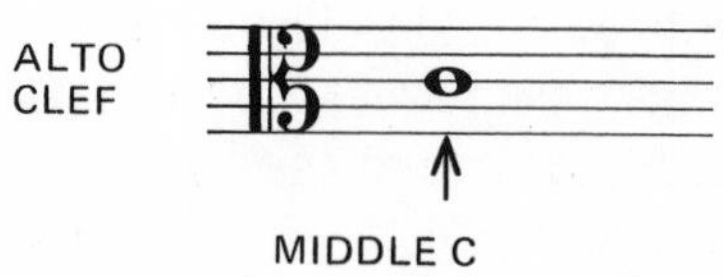

ALTO CLEF — MIDDLE C   TENOR CLEF — MIDDLE C   83

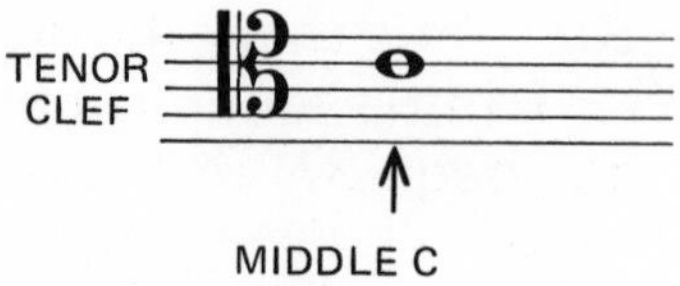

Chord.   The sound of two or more notes being played or sung together.   50-52

Chord Shapes.   The diagrams, often shown above the Stave, which give the fingering for chords on the guitar, piano, organ and other instruments.   50

Chord Symbols.   The names given to chords — C, Am, G7, and so on.   50

Chorus.   The part of a piece of music where everyone joins in and plays or sings together.
A group of singers and the music written for them.

Clef.   A sign at the beginning of each Stave which indicates the names and positions of notes.
The Treble or G Clef indicates the note G above Middle C.

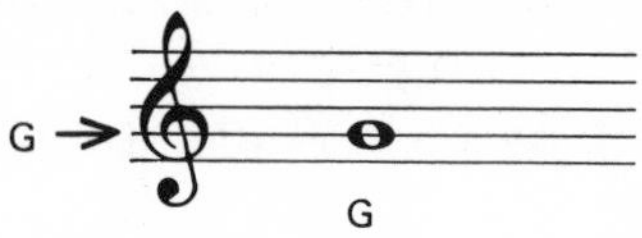

G   10-11

The Bass or F Clef indicates the note F below Middle C.

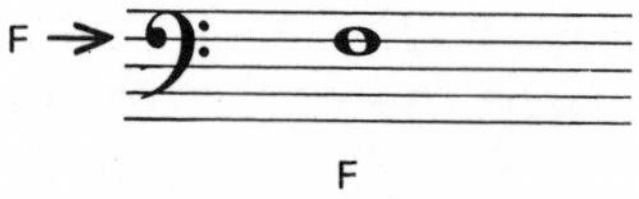

F   10-11

The C Clef indicates the note Middle C in two positions. On the middle line it is known as the Alto Clef, on the fourth line it is known as the Tenor Clef.

ALTO CLEF — MIDDLE C   TENOR CLEF — MIDDLE C   83

Coda   (It.).   The Coda is the 'tail' of a piece of music — an extra few bars added to the end. It is often marked by the sign ⊕ .   45

Coll, Coll', Colla   (It.).   With the.

Common Time. Music with 2, 4, 8 or 16 beats to the bar. Music with a $\frac{4}{4}$ or **C** Time Signature is often said to be in Common Time.   24-25

Compound Time Signatures.   see pages   61-63

Con (It.). With.

Con anima (It.). With movement.

Con amore (It.). With love, with tenderness.

Con Forza (It). With force, strongly.

Con moto (It.). With movement.

Con Sordini (It.). With mutes. Mutes make an instrument quieter and change the character of the tone.

Con 8ve, con 8, under a note, means that the written note *and* the note with the same name an Octave lower are to be played at the same time.   75-76

Contradict. In a musical sense, contradict means 'cancel the effect of'. A Natural sign contradicts (cancels the effect of) an Accidental Sharp or Flat sign.   32

Contralto or Alto. The lowest voices of women and boys.

Couplet or Duplet. Two notes which fit into the time of three notes of the same type (or value). They are shown grouped together by a curved line and the figure 2 —   79

Crescendo, cres. (It.). Increasing. Gradually become louder. Usually marked with the sign $\diagdown$.   43

Crotchet or Quarter Note. A quarter of a Whole Note. It is written $\downarrow$ or $\uparrow$.   14 & 87

A Crotchet (or Quarter Note) Rest is written ξ or $\uparrow$.   20

Da Capo, D.C. (It.). Repeat from the beginning.   45

Da Capo al Fine (It.). Repeat the whole piece of music from the beginning as far as the word 'Fine'.   45

Dal Segno, D.S. (It.). Repeat from the sign — $\%$.   45

Dash. The sign (ˈ) above or below a note. The note marked should be very short and sharply played.   77

D.C., Da Capo (It.). Repeat from the beginning.   45

Decrescendo, decres. (It.). Decrease. Gradually become softer. Usually marked with this sign: $\diagup$.

Demi-semiquaver or Thirty-second Note. One thirty-second of a Whole Note. It is written $\backslash$ OR $\upharpoonright$ Two or more may be joined together — . The Demi-semiquaver Rest is written — $\frac{?}{?}$.   57

Descant.   An extra 'counter melody' added above the melody.

Diminuendo, dim.   (It.).   Diminishing. Gradually become softer. Usually marked with the sign $\diagdown$.   43

Divisi   (It.).   Divided. The music is to divide into separate parts after a period of Unison (where everyone was playing or singing the same notes).

Dolce   (It.).   Sweetly.

Doppio movimento   (It.).   Twice as fast. At double speed.

Dots.

A small dot after a note or rest means it is to last half as long again. (One and a half times its normal length.)

$$\textit{d.} = \textit{d} + \textit{d} \, , \quad \textit{d.} = \textit{d} + \textit{d} \, , \quad \textit{d.} = \textit{d} + \textit{d} \, , \quad \textit{d.} = \textit{d} + \textit{d}$$

Occasionally, more than one dot may be used. Then each extra dot adds half as much as the previous dot:

$$\textit{d..} = \textit{d} + \textit{d} + \textit{d} \, , \qquad \textit{d...} = \textit{d} + \textit{d} + \textit{d} + \textit{d}$$ 22

A dot over or under notes ($\textit{d}$ $\textit{p}$) means they should be short

and sharp with a silent space between each note and the next. This is called 'Staccato'.   77

Double Bar-Line.   DOUBLE BAR-LINES

Double Bar-lines mark the end of a piece of music. They may   15
also divide music into sections, mark Repeats (see page 44), changes of Key (see page 37) or a change of Time Signature (see page 63).

Double Flat.   The $\flat\flat$ sign which further flattens a note which is already Flat.   69

Double Sharp.   The **x** sign which further sharpens a note which is already Sharp.   68

D.S., Dal Segno   (It.).   Repeat from the sign— $\%$.   45

D.S. Al Coda   (It.).   Repeat the music from the sign $\%$ until you come to 'Al Coda $\oplus$ ', then go to the Coda ($\oplus$).   45

Duet or **Duo.**   A group of two players or singers, or a piece of music for two performers.

Duple Time.   Music with two beats to the bar. $\frac{2}{2}$, $\frac{2}{4}$, $\frac{2}{8}$ are Simple Duple Time. $\frac{6}{4}$, $\frac{6}{8}$, $\frac{6}{16}$ are Compound Duple Time with two main, accented beats to the bar.   60-62

Duplet or Couplet. Two notes which fit into the time of three notes of the same type (or value). They are shown grouped together by a curved line and the figure 2.   79

E or **ed**   (It.).   And.

Eighth Note or Quaver.   An eighth of a Whole Note.

It is written ♪ or ♪ . Two or more may be joined together — ♫ .   14 & 87

An Eighth Note (or Quaver) Rest is written ♵ .   20

F Clef.   The Bass Clef which gives the position of the note F below Middle C.   ← F   10-11

Fermata, Fermato   (It.).   Pause. Usually shown with this sign ⌢ .   42

Fine   (It.).   Finish, the end. Often used to mark the place where the music is to finish after Repeats.   45

Flat.   The Flat sign (♭) lowers a note — the Flat note below is played or sung instead of the Natural note with the same letter name. B Flat (written B♭) is the Flat note below B.

B   B♭

Flats may be part of the Key Signature at the beginning of every line of music (see pages 34 and 70), or written in front of notes which are to be changed as 'Accidentals'.   30

F Flat and C Flat are the notes normally known as E Natural and B Natural.   69

Forte   (It.).   Loudly. Usually shown as f .   43

Fortepiano   (It.).   A sudden change from loud to soft. Usually shown as fp .   43

Fortissimo   (It.).   Very loudly. Usually shown as ff .   43

Fortississimo   (It.).   As loudly as possible. Usually shown as fff .   43

Forza   (It.).   Force, strength. (Con forza = strongly.)

Fuoco   (It.).   Fire.

G Clef.   The Treble Clef which gives the position of the note G above Middle C.

← G   10-11

Giocoso   (It.).   Humorously.

Giusto   (It.).   In exact time. At the proper speed.

Glissando, gliss.   (It.).   Sliding. On the piano or organ, white notes are played one after the other by quickly running the back of the finger up the keyboard. A similar effect is often used on the harp by making a stroke across the strings. On stringed instruments, the guitar and other fretted instruments, it is made by sliding the finger up or down a string after a note has been played.

Grace Notes, Graces.   Decorations or Ornaments added to music.   77

Grandioso   (It.).   Grandly.

Grave   (It.).   Slow, solemn and dignified.

Grazia   (It.).   Grace.

Grazioso   (It.).   Gracefully.

Gusto   (It.).   Enjoyment, zest.

Half Note or Minim.   Half a Whole Note. It is written $\downarrow$ or $\upharpoonleft$.   14 & 87
   The Half Note (or Minim) Rest is written

   20

Hold or Pause.   The sign $\frown$ over a note, chord or rest means it is to last for more than its normal length. The actual length is left for the player, singer or leader of the choir or orchestra to decide. Over a Double Bar-Line it marks the place where the music is to finish.   42 & 45

Key.   Music is said to be in a particular Key when it is based upon the Scale starting with the Key Note of the same name — Music in the Key of C Major is based upon the Scale of C Major.   34

Key Note.   The starting note of a Scale. Key Signatures and Scales are named after their Key Note.   34

Key Signatures.   Sharp ($\sharp$) and Flat ($\flat$) signs shown on the Stave immediately after the Clef. The Sharp and Flat signs in the Key Signature affect all notes with the same name as the ones marked in the music — except where Accidental Sharp, Flat or Natural ($\natural$) signs are written in, or a new Key Signature occurs. The Key Signature for C Major and A Minor has no Sharps or Flats.   34 & 70

Larghetto   (It.).   Rather slowly, but not as slow as 'Largo'.

Largo   (It.).   Slow and dignified.

Legato, Leg.   (It.).   Smooth. Music marked Legato should be played or sung very smoothly.

Leger Lines.   Short lines written in when needed for notes which are above or below the Stave.   17 & 93

Leggiero (It.).   Lightly.

Lento (It.).   Very slow.

Loco (Lat.).   In place. Occasionally used after an Octave sign (8ve). It means that the notes are to be played or sung as written from that point onwards. 76

Lyrics.   The words to a song.

Maestoso (It.).   Grandly, majestically.

Major Chords. see page   51

Major Keys. see pages   34 & 70

Major Scales. see pages   34 & 70

Manuscript, M.S.   A piece of music which is hand written and not printed. Manuscript Paper and Manuscript Books have blank Staves on which you can write your own music.

Marcato, Marc. (It.).   Marked, accented, distinct.

Marcia (It.).   A March, a piece of military music.

Measure or Bar.   The space between two Bar-Lines.

← A BAR OR →
MEASURE 15

Melody.   The tune.

Meno (It.).   Less. Meno mosso = less movement, slower.

Metronome.   A clockwork instrument for setting the Tempo (speed) of music. It can be set to tick at various speeds and is used when an exact number of beats to the minute is required. see page   42

Mezzo (It.).   Half, medium, often shown as *m*.

Mezzo-Forte (It.).   Moderately loudly, usually shown as *mf*.

Mezzo-Piano (It.).   Moderately softly, usually shown as *mp*. 43

Mezzo Voce (It.).   Half voice — softer than normal singing.

Middle C.   The note C, roughly in the middle of the piano, and roughly in the middle of the range of human voices. It is written on the Stave in these positions:

MIDDLE C   MIDDLE C   MIDDLE C   MIDDLE C

Minim or Half Note.   Half a Whole Note. It is written 𝅗𝅥 or 𝅗𝅥.
The Minim (or Half Note) Rest is written: 14 & 87

20

Minor Chords. see page   51

Minor Keys. see pages   65 & 70

Minor Scales. see pages   65 & 70

Moderato, mod.   (It.).   Moderately, medium Tempo (speed).

Molto   (It.).   Very. Molto allegro = very fast.

Mordent.   Two note melodic Ornaments indicated by these signs:
ᨠ   ᨠ   see page   79

Morendo, Mor.   (It.).   Dying away at the end.

Mosso   (It.).   Movement. Più mosso = more movement, quicker. Meno mosso = less movement, slower.

Moto   (It.).   Movement. Con Moto = with movement.

M.S., M.S.S.   Manuscript, manuscripts. Music written by hand and not printed.

Natural Note.   A note which is not Sharp or Flat. A, B, C, D, E, F, G are Natural Notes.

Natural Sign.   The Natural sign (♮) in front of a note contradicts (cancels) the effect of an Accidental Sharp (♯) or Flat (♭) sign — or Sharp or Flat signs in the Key Signature. A Natural note is then played or sung instead of the Sharp or Flat note.   32

Non   (It.).   Not. Non troppo = not too much.

Notation.   The name given to ways of writing music.

Note.   A musical sound. A sign which represents a musical sound.

Octave.   An Octave covers the eight notes of any Scale. It is the distance between any note and the next note higher or lower which has the same name. C to the next C higher or lower is an Octave —

C   D   E   F   G   A   B   C
1   2   3   4   5   6   7   8

The second C is an OCTAVE HIGHER than the first C.

The first C is an OCTAVE LOWER than the second.

Octave may also refer to all the notes — Naturals, Sharps or Flats between two notes with the same name an Octave apart.   75

The Octave sign — 8ve, 8va or 8 . . . over notes means they should be played or sung an Octave higher than written.

Under notes, the Octave sign means they should be played or sung an Octave lower.   76

Con 8 or Con 8ve under a note means that the written note *and* the note with the same name an Octave below are to be played at the same time.   76

The 'range' of musical instruments and voices is usually described by the number of Octaves able to be played or sung.   76

Music for the guitar, double bass and some other instruments is always written an Octave higher than it sounds to make it easier to read. Tenor voice parts are often written an Octave higher and shown on the Treble Clef (𝄞). Other music may be written higher or lower than it sounds to make it easier to read. 12 & 94

Opus, Op. Work. 'Opus' is used to describe the order in which the work of a composer was published. Opus 1 is the first piece published by a composer, Opus 2 is the second, and so on.

Ornaments. Musical decorations or 'Grace Notes'. see pages 77-79

Part. Music for a particular instrument or voice in a band, group, orchestra or choir. 46

Pause or Hold. The Pause sign 𝄐 over a note, chord or rest means it is to last for more than its normal length. The actual length is left for the player, singer or leader of the orchestra or choir to decide. The sign may also mark a pause in the music. Over a Double Bar-Line it marks the end of the music. 42

Pedal, Ped. On piano music, Ped. means that the right (sustaining) pedal should be pressed down. A line (________) under notes often shows how long it is to be pressed. An asterisk (*) may be used to mark where the pedal is to be lifted. Breaks in the line mean it is to be lifted, but pressed down again (___/____/__).

Perdendosi, Perd. (It.). Losing itself, dying away.

Pianissimo (It.). Very soft. Usually shown as ***pp***.

Pianississimo (It.). As quietly as possible. Usually shown as ***ppp***. 43

Piano (It.). Soft. Usually shown as ***p*** .

Pianoforte (It.). The proper name for a piano.

Phrase. In music, a phrase is similar to a line of poetry. It is a continuous length of melody or harmony usually several bars long.

Pitch. The height or depth of a sound.

Più (It.). More. Più allegro = a little faster. Più Mosso = more movement, a little quicker.

Più Forte (It.). More loudly. Usually shown as ***pf***. 43

Pizzicato, Pizz. (It.). Stringed instruments should be plucked instead of bowed.

Poco (It.). Little.

Poco a Poco (It.). Little by little. Cres. poco a poco = get louder very gradually.

Pomposo (It.). Pompously, very dignified.

Prestissimo (It.). Very, very quickly.

Presto (It.). Very quickly.

Quadruple Time. Music with four beats to the bar. $\frac{4}{2}$, $\frac{4}{4}$, $\frac{4}{8}$, and so on are Simple Quadruple Time. $\frac{12}{4}$, $\frac{12}{8}$, $\frac{12}{16}$, are Compound Quadruple Time, with four main accented beats to the bar. 60-63

Quadruplet. Four notes which fit into the time of six notes of the same type (or value). They are shown grouped together by a line and the figure 4:

79

Quarter Note or Crotchet. A quarter of a Whole Note. It is written ♩ or ♩ . A Quarter Note (or Crotchet) Rest is written 𝄽 or 𝄽 .

14 & 87

Quartet. A group of four singers or players, or a piece of music for four performers.

Quaver or Eighth Note. An eighth of a Whole Note.
It is written ♪ or ♪ . Two or more may be joined together: ♫

14 & 87

The Quaver (or Eighth Note) Rest is written: 𝄾.

20

Quintet. A group of five players or singers, or a piece of music for five performers.

Quintruplet. Five notes which fit into the time of four notes of the same type (or value). They are shown grouped together with a line and the figure 5:

79

Rallentando, rall. (It.). Slow down gradually.

42

Refrain. The chorus, or a part of a piece of music which recurs several times.

Relative Major and Relative Minor. The two Keys, one Major and one Minor, which have the same Key Signature.

65 & 70

Repeats. The Repeat sign 𝄇 — a Double Bar-Line with two dots — means that the music is to be repeated from a similar sign facing the other way — 𝄆 , or from the beginning if there is no other sign.

Other words and signs may also indicate a repeat.   see pages

44-45

Chord Symbols which are to be repeated are often shown by a stroke (╱). One stroke is used each time the chord is repeated.

52

Single Notes, Rests and Bars which are to be repeated are shown by strokes (╱) used in various ways.

80-82

Rests. Signs which indicate a period of silence. Rests are named after the notes which they replace, and are counted in the same way as these notes.   see pages

20 & 57

Rinforzando, rinf. (It.). Give extra emphasis. Also shown as *rf* .

Ritardando, ritard. (It.). Slow down gradually. 42
Ritenuto, Rit. (It.). Held back — slightly slower.
Run. A series of notes, usually part of a Scale, which is played or
sung quickly.

Scale A series of notes in alphabetical order, starting with the
Key Note after which the Scale is named.
Major Scales see pages 34 & 70
Minor Scales see pages 65 & 70
Score. All the Parts for the different instruments and voices needed
in a piece of music shown together, one above the other on the
same page.
A Full (or Open) Score for an orchestra or choir has a separate
Stave for each instrument and voice.
A Vocal Score gives each Voice Part a separate Stave, but has
the Parts for the accompanying instruments on two Staves only.
A Short Score gives the Parts for all voices or instruments on
two Staves, to save space and be more convenient to handle. 49
Segue (It.). Follow on at once without a break.
Semibreve or Whole Note. This is the longest note normally used.
It is written **o** . The Semibreve (or Whole Note) Rest is written :

This rest is also used where there is to be a whole bar's rest. 14 & 87
Semi-demi-semiquaver or Sixty-Fourth Note. This is the very
rarely used shortest note. One sixty-fourth of a Whole Note, it is
written ♬ or ♬ . Two or more may be joined together: 57

A Semi-demi-semiquaver (or Sixty-Fourth Note) Rest is written: 57

Semiquaver or Sixteenth Note. One Sixteenth of a Whole Note. It is
written ♪ or ♪ . Two or more may be joined together: 56 & 87

The Semiquaver (or Sixteenth Note) Rest is written: ♪ . 57

Semitone. The smallest distance from one note to another in
written music. It is the distance from any note to the next note
higher or lower —
A Sharp note is one Semitone higher than the Natural note with
the same letter name — G Sharp is one Semitone above G.
A Flat note is one Semitone lower than the Natural note with the
same letter name — B Flat is one Semitone below B.
E to F is one Semitone; B to C is one Semitone. (continued overleaf)

107

On the guitar and most fretted instruments, the note on each fret is one Semitone higher than the fret below:

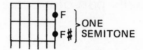

On the keyboard, the next note higher, black or white, is one Semitone higher, and so on. A Tone is two Semitones.

Sempre, semp. (It.). Always.

Senza (It.). Without.

Sextuplet or Sextolet. Six notes which fit into the time of four notes of the same type (or value). They are shown grouped together by a line and the figure 6.

79

Sforzando, sf, sfz. (It.). The note or chord marked is to be given special emphasis. 77

Shake or Trill. A two-note melodic ornament indicated by one of these signs: *tr* or *tr* 〰〰 see page 78

Sharp. The Sharp sign (♯) raises a note — the Sharp note above is played or sung instead of the Natural note with the same name. C Sharp (written C♯) is the Sharp note above C.

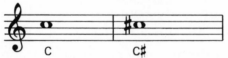

Sharps may be part of the Key Signatures at the beginning of every line of music (see pages 34 and 70), or written in front of notes which are to be changed as 'Accidentals'. 28

E Sharp and B Sharp are the notes normally known as F Natural and C Natural. 68

Signature. There are two Signatures: Key Signatures. see pages 34 & 70

Time Signatures. see pages 24 & 60

Simple Time Signatures. see page 60

Sixteenth Note or Semiquaver. One sixteenth of a Whole Note. It is written ♬ or ♬ . Two or more may be joined together: ♫ 56 & 87

The Sixteenth Note (or Semiquaver) Rest is written: ♪ 57

Sixty-Fourth Note or Semi-demi-semiquaver. This is the very rarely used shortest note. One sixty-fourth of a Whole Note, it is written ♬ or ♬ . Two or more may be joined together: ♬ . 57

A Sixty-Fourth Note (or Semi-demi-semiquaver) Rest is written: ♪ 57

Slur. A curved line over (⌒) or under (⌣) several different notes means they are to be played or sung smoothly. Slurs also show musical phrases, the 'bowing' of stringed instruments and the way words fit into songs.   21

When two different notes are joined by a Slur, the second note is to be slightly shorter and weaker than the first. A Slur over 'Staccato' notes means that they are to be less Staccato.   77

Solo (It.). Music for one instrument or singer. Also a piece of music, or a part of it, which displays the performance of one player or singer.

Soprano or Treble. The higher voices of women and boys. Also, instruments which play the notes of these voices.

Sordino, Sordini (It.). Mute, mutes. Mutes make an instrument quieter and change the character of the tone.

Sostenuto, sost. (It.). Sustained, held. The note marked should be given its full length.

Sotto (It.). Under, below. 8va sotto = play or sing an Octave lower.

Sotto Voce (It.). In a low voice. The music is to be performed in a quiet subdued manner.

Staccato, stacc. (It.). Detached. Staccato notes are played or sung short and sharp with a silent space between each note. Staccato is indicated by a dot above or below a note:

    77

Stave or Staff. The five lines and four spaces on which music is written.   10

Syncopation. Cross rhythms which occur when notes which would normally be weak are given strong accents.

Tablature, TAB. An old-fashioned method of writing music. Some music for the guitar and lute is still written in Tablature using a Stave with a line for each string. Numbers, letters or note signs on each line indicate when, and how each string is to be played.

Tacet (Lat.). Be silent. The voice or instrument marked is to be silent.

Tempo (It.). The speed of music.   41-42
'Tempo di Valse' is Waltz Time.
'A Tempo' means play or sing in time, or go back to original speed.

Tenor. The higher voices of men. Also instruments which play the notes of these voices.

Tenor Clef.   The C Clef giving the position of the note Middle C on the fourth line of the Stave.

83

Tenuto, ten.   (It.).   Hold, sustain. The note marked should be given its full length.

Thirty-Second Note or Demi-semiquaver.   One thirty-second of a Whole Note, and half a Sixteenth Note. It is written ♪ or ♪.

57 & 87

Two or more may be joined together:

The Thirty-Second Note (or Demi-semiquaver) Rest is written: ♪

57

Tie or Bind.   A curved line (⌣ or ⌢) which lengthens a note by joining it to the next note — if the notes have the same name and position on the Stave. The first note lasts for the combined number of beats of the notes 'tied' together.
A curved line which links different notes is not a Tie, but a Slur (see pages 21 and 77).

21

Time.   Time refers to the number of beats in a bar, not the speed of music. The Time of music is shown by Time Signatures.

Time Signatures.   Two numbers or a sign on the Stave at the beginning of music. The top number gives the number of beats in a bar, the bottom number gives the type (or value) of the beats — 2̄ for Half Notes, 4̄ for Quarter Notes, 8̄ for Eighth Notes, and so on.

Number of beats (2)
Type of beats (4 = Quarter Notes) ➝ $\frac{2}{4}$

$\frac{4}{4}$ is often written ' **C** ' and $\frac{2}{2}$ is often written ' **₵** '.

Time Signatures refer to the number of beats, not the number of notes in a bar. They do not refer to the speed of the music. Along with other signs, Time Signatures give the rhythm of music.

24 & 60

Tone.   (1).   A Tone is two Semitones.   see 'Semitone'

107

Tone.   (2).   The Quality of sound made by a voice or instrument.

Tonic.   Another name for the Key Note — the starting note of a Scale after which the Key and Key Signature are named.

35

Top Line.   The melody or tune.

47

Tranquillo   (It.).   Tranquil, calmly.

Transposing.   Rewriting music in a different Key or different Octave.

Transposing Instruments. Instruments whose music is written in one Key, but sounds in another. Music for the B♭ clarinet sounds in B♭ when it is written in C. 49

Treble or Soprano. The higher voices of women and boys. Also instruments which play the notes of these voices.

Treble Clef. The G Clef which gives the position of the note G above Middle C.

← G 10-11

Tre Corde. In piano music, it means the left (soft) pedal is to be released following a section marked 'Una Corda'.

Tremolo, trem. (It.). The notes marked are to be repeated many times as quickly as possible without worrying about the exact number of notes played. see page 82

Trill or Shake. A two-note melodic ornament indicated by one of these signs: *tr* or *tr* ⌇⌇ 78

Trio. A group of three players or singers, or a piece of music for three performers.

Triple Time. Music with three beats to the bar. $\frac{3}{2}$, $\frac{3}{4}$, $\frac{3}{8}$, and so on are Simple Triple Time. $\frac{9}{4}$, $\frac{9}{8}$, $\frac{9}{16}$ are Compound Triple Time with three main accented beats to the bar. 60-62

Triplet. Three notes which fit into the time of two notes of the same type (or value). They are shown grouped together by a line and the figure 3:

see page 58

Troppo (It.). Much. Non troppo = not too much, not too . . .

Turn. A four note melodic ornament, indicated by signs ∾ or ⌒ . Inverted Turns are marked ↲ , ⌒ , ∾ or § see page 78

Tutti (It.). All. Everyone is to play or sing.

Una Corda (It.). In piano music, the left (soft) pedal is to be pressed down.

Unison. Two or more instruments or voices playing or singing the same notes.

Valse. A Waltz.

Vibrato (It.). A slight wavering (or vibration) of a note. This is a technique particularly used in singing. On string instruments, it is produced by vibrating the finger on a string while a note is being played.

Vivace (It.). Lively.

Vivo (It.). Alive.

Voce (It.). Voice.

Volti Subito, V.S. (It.). Turn the page over quickly.

Waltz. Music with three beats to the bar. A Waltz is a dance to music with three beats to the bar.   25

Whole Note or Semibreve. The longest note which is normally used. It is written **o** . The Whole Note (or Semibreve) Rest is written: 14 & 87

This rest is also used where there is to be a whole bar of silence.   20

MUSIC IN THIS BOOK   PAGE

All arranged by Roger Evans.